ZEN
BEYOND
ALL WORDS

ZEN
BEYOND
ALL WORDS

*A Western
Zen Master's
Instructions*

Wolfgang Kopp

*Translated by
Barbara Wittenberg-Hasenauer*

Charles E. Tuttle Co., Inc.
Boston • Rutland, Vermont • Tokyo

First published in the United States in 1996 by Charles E. Tuttle Co., Inc.
of Rutland, Vermont, and Tokyo, Japan, with editorial offices at
153 Milk Street, Boston, Massachusetts 02109.

First published in German in 1993
by Ansata-Verlag Interlaken, Switzerland.
© 1993 Wolfgang Kopp
translation © 1996 Ansata-Verlag

Library of Congress Cataloging-in-Publication Data

Kopp, Wolfgang, 1938–
    Zen beyond all words : a western Zen master's instructions /
Wolfgang Kopp ; translated by Barbara Wittenberg-Hasenauer.
        p.   cm.   — (Tuttle library of enlightenment)
    ISBN 0-8048-3086-X
    1. Spiritual life—Zen Buddhism. 2. Zen Buddhism—Doctrines.
I. Wittenberg-Hasenauer, Barbara. II. Title. III. Series.
BQ9288.K67 1996
294.3'4—dc20   96-5155
                                                         CIP

First edition

1 3 5 7 9 10 8 6 4 2

97 99 01 00 98 97 96

Printed in the United States of America

Heartfelt thanks to all my students who took part in the preparation and editing of this book.

This book is dedicated in loving gratitude to my master Soji Enku, Roshi, who died in 1977.

—*Wolfgang Kopp*

Contents

Editors' Foreword

This book contains a selection of talks given by Master Wolfgang Kopp at the Tao Ch'an Center in Wiesbaden, Germany, during the summer of 1992.

In the spirit of the ancient Chinese Ch'an masters, Wolfgang Kopp teaches a direct and powerful Zen. He conveys neither a theoretical system nor a one-sided dogmatism of sitting, and he neither wears customary robes nor holds a traditional title.

His sole aim is our liberation from old patterns of behavior and modes of thought, leading ultimately to the enlightenment of the mind. He uses all means to awaken us out of the slumber of habit, because habit, regardless of its form, hinders us from directly experiencing reality. On every page of this book the

Master shows us the mirror of our true being, and in it we recognize our ever-present buddha-nature, our original state of enlightenment.

Time and again Master Kopp stresses that the truth cannot be expressed in words—that it is *beyond all words*. Nonetheless words guide us, just as does the finger that points to the moon. We must only take care not to cling to the finger and mistake it for the moon itself.

Wolfgang Kopp's humorous, yet powerful and direct style of teaching lends his talks incredible liveliness. Take, for example, the way in which he illuminates a saying of an ancient Chinese Zen master. He seizes on a profound thought and then makes an unexpected comparison to everyday life or uses an anecdote to reveal its meaning.

In Wolfgang Kopp's talks we can sense the realization of a great enlightened master. His energy-packed words of shocking openness are filled with such spiritual power that they can strike us like a flash of lightning. They often shatter the logic of our conceptual, discriminating thinking to enable us to grasp the truth *beyond all words*.

With the publication of these talks, we hope that this book will reach the hands of all who are spiritually ripe for the teaching of one of the greatest spiritual masters of our times.

The editors
Tao Ch'an Center, Wiesbaden

Zen is *beyond all words.*
Away with all thinking and explaining.
There is only mysterious silent understanding
and no more.

—Zen Master Huang-po

The Treasure House Within You

The transitory nature of all existence can suddenly and unexpectedly shatter all your speculations. That's why I advise you: It's best not to cultivate any intentions. Anything you've ever begun is an activity with some objective, yet in the face of death it has no value whatsoever.

But don't mistake my words to mean that you should refrain from undertaking any further activities, that it's better to withdraw and live a solitary life far away from the hustle and bustle of the world. Many people seriously believe that such behavior is the guarantee for a spiritual life, but they are gravely mistaken. The important thing is that you learn to do the things that must be done, without letting things have control over you. You must learn how to handle things, possess things, without letting things possess *you;* you must act, but be inwardly free of your action. This is true living by Zen. "When the occasion arises to act, then act; when the occasion passes, then remain quiescent," Huang-po tells us.

A student goes to his master and asks, "Master, what is your Zen (meaning: What is your way of living by Zen)?" And the Master says, "When I'm hungry, I eat, and when I'm tired, I sleep." "Yes," says the monk, "that's fine, but we do that too. What's so special about it?" "Well," says the Master, "when you eat, you think a thousand thoughts that take you here and there, and when you sleep, fears and wishes fill your dreams. But when I eat, I just eat. And when I sleep, I just sleep. That is my Zen."

This reveals the simplicity of Zen—the simplicity of the pure truth itself. Zen is the pinnacle and quintessence of all Buddhism. It's the quickest path to liberation from being caught in *samsara,* the cycle of birth and death. I term Zen and the pure unadulterated truth as *one.* All else that is not the pure truth is dogmatism and the acrobatic speculation of the brain—a heap of intellectual scrap. It's a cover, a shadow overlying reality and thus of no value.

The truth of Zen is simple and direct. A Zen student comes to his master and asks, "Master, I can't tell the difference between black and white. What do you say to that?" The Master says, "Please come a bit closer. I can't hear well today." The student steps closer and repeats himself: "Master, I can't tell the difference between black and white." Hardly has he spoken these words when he receives a ringing blow to the ear. The student bows and says, "Now I know." He is enlightened on the spot.

That's it. Why make it complicated? It's so easy. But because it's so easy, you make it complicated. Why? Because for so long you have believed that anything of any value can only be gained through much exertion and effort. But there is nothing to gain, really nothing—absolutely nothing! "Do you seek the truth, do you seek Tao?" asks Zen. "Then simply look around and realize that you are standing in the midst of it." Reality is *here* and nowhere else! Zen Master Lin-chi, Huang-po's dharma heir, says: "You wear out your feet rushing around in all directions; what do you seek? There is no Buddha to seek, nor Tao to perfect, nor dharma to attain."

No sooner do you hear of enlightenment, of Zen, and of a higher reality that transcends death than you set about your search. But Zen says there is no Buddha to seek, nor Tao to perfect, nor *dharma* (truth) to attain. The Buddha or reality you seek can only be found *within* you. Tao is the way, and Tao is reality. It's like a river: It flows, and when you are one with Tao, you are like a rubber ball floating on the surface. When the wave swells, you go up with it, and when the wave subsides, you go down with it; when the wave rises and is born, you are one with it, and when the wave dies, you are also one with it. Everything is good just as it is.

"There is no law to attain," says Huang-po, meaning there is no divine universal rule in the form of "you must do this or that." Every religion, be it Jewish, Muslim, Christian, or Hindu, has its rules and specific laws and guidelines that must be followed. Followers believe that unless they obey these laws and live in strict adherence to the moral code and rules, they'll be unable to enter the kingdom of God. What a mistake! There is no divine reality to enter or seek because it's already present, it's *within you!* In the words of the eighth-century Chinese Zen Master Da-zhu, "The treasure house within you contains everything and you are free to use it. You don't need to seek outside."

You're conditioned by your upbringing and by all the various influences of Christian culture with respect to your notion of divine reality. You also have a very specific concept of the religious realization you're attempting to achieve. However, Zen says: "The real Buddha has no form, the real Tao has no appearance,

3

the true law has no exterior signs." The true law, according to Buddhist teaching, stands for *dharma*—the universal law—and refers to the manifestation of the universal truth through Buddha or the buddhas, the enlightened masters.

This true dharma, this true revelation of reality, has no exterior signs. If you were to notice even a single sign of any sort, it would be proof against it being the true dharma. The *true law*, the true revelation of Zen, is the *nonlaw*, beyond words, beyond comprehension. Buddha, Tao, and the true law are all *one*. There's no multiplicity. The reality on which all is grounded, the way you follow to attain this reality, and the true dharma as the manifestation of the divine are all one and the same. People who don't grasp this block their way to any realization. They just turn in circles and seek and analyze and poke about here and there with the hope of finding something. Somewhere they believe they'll come across some great philosophical knowledge that will make everything clear from the outside. Zen, however, rises above all of this.

If you can keep your thoughts from rambling, you're well on the path to liberation. Believe me, there's nothing to be gained from the outside. Why concern yourself with all sorts of intellectual rubbish? What's the point of rooting around in every corner like a dog who scarfs up nothing but old trash in its muzzle? Dip into your own treasure, for the truth you seek is closer to you than you are to yourself. *There is nothing to seek!* There is no space in which things are separate from each other, and there is no time when something not yet, or no longer, is. Everything is *simultaneous*. Everything is *here* and *now!*

This, too, is the central thought of the Hua-yen school of Chinese Buddhism, which is based on the *Avatamsaka Sutra*. The foundation of Hua-yen is the teaching of the mutual penetration of all things, the teaching of the fundamental oneness and sameness of all being. The whole universe is a total organism, a cosmic network, in which everything mutually penetrates and is connected to everything else. To better illustrate this the *Avatam-saka Sutra* uses the analogy of Indra's pearl net.

The sutra says that a great pearl net hangs high up in the heavens above the palace of the god Indra. All the pearls in this net are strung in such a way that each pearl reflects all the other pearls. Thus a single pearl contains all the others and at the same time mirrors, through the reflection of light, the entire cosmos with everything in it. Everything is an all-encompassing totality in which all is contained. Everything is an absolute *here* and *now.*

Because everything is *here* and *now,* where and what do you seek? "Now is here and here is now!" If you want to experience the reality of your being, you must thoroughly immerse yourself in this *now* and in this *here.* How else can you experience *here* except *now?* How can you experience *now* when you are caught up in tomorrow or the day after tomorrow, when your thoughts are scattered here and there? Once again we return to "*mu—nothing.*" Mu is *nothing* in relation to space and time—and thus *nothing* with regard to the contents of all consciousness.

Mu is *here-now!* It's where there is no coming and no going. Mu is behind, in front, above, below, and to the side—everywhere, all-encompassing. This mu is now! And this *now* is eternity. Realize this and thoroughly immerse yourselves in it!

Why can't you realize your original nature when it's always present? Why do you cling to all sorts of "spiritual disciplines" that are merely pastimes of the ego and of no value? I don't teach the currently widespread, dead Zen of suppressing your thoughts while sitting bolt-upright with your eyes closed. At this instant, be *now* entirely *here* and see things just as they are. Be independent of everything, and you will attain all-encompassing realization in a flash.

A highbrow theologian once came to my master Soji Enku and said, "I heard your last lecture; however I'm still not clear on the facts of Zen. I would therefore like to ask you: What is the truth of Zen?" And Soji Enku said simply, "The ground beneath your feet; that is the truth of Zen." Everything is utterly clear, but things become cloudy as a result of your projections. You will never find entry to the truth of Zen as long as you are a prisoner of your intellect and use your brain to try to figure things out. That reminds me of another little incident I experienced with Soji Enku that I'd like to tell you about.

One afternoon a number of students sat together with him in his study. Soji Enku reclined in his desk chair. Everyone was busy talking except the Master, who said nothing and had so completely withdrawn himself that hardly anyone noticed him. He just sat there quietly, apparently not participating, yet observing everything. Suddenly he pointed to the wall and said, "Look at that! What's that nasty spot there? Where did it come from all of a sudden?" All the students looked and asked "What spot?" "Over there," the Master said. "Don't you see it? There's a spot right there." "No, we don't see any spot." "But I see it! That spot really annoys me." All at once Soji Enku took off his glasses and said, "Oh, it's gone. What happened to the spot?" He put his glasses back on and said, "What on earth! Now it's back." He then examined his glasses and said, "Oh, what's that spot on my glasses?" Afterwards everyone was sheepish and quiet because they all understood the lesson. Together they'd filled the room with their individual projections in terms of ideas, identifications, and misinterpretations. One idea confronted another idea, ignorance confronted ignorance. Much ado about nothing.

You are deceived by the world of illusion, *maya,* which is a phenomenon having no reality of its own. Your only choice is to leave everything as it is, let everything go, and detach yourselves from everything. Free yourselves of everything, and that which *is* and always *was* will dawn bright and clear.

Enlightenment doesn't come in from the outside. Lots of people think it's possible to sit around in ignorance and wait for a light to come on suddenly like a light bulb, making everything clear. What really happens is that the projections you've been casting over reality for incarnations too numerous to mention melt away on their own. The result is that everything is just as it is and always was. You'll find there is no such thing as birth and death and there is no space and time dimension to life. These are just parts of the dream of maya that you yourselves dream—they are projections of ignorance.

Enlightenment and nonenlightenment, being caught in the cycle of birth and death; old age, despair, sickness, pain, and death are all part of your dream. That's why there's only *one* way out and that is: *Wake up!* Wake up and stop dreaming!

[Short silence]

Should I say more? Or should I stop here? If I stop here, you're in danger of believing that all that needs to be said about the truth has been said. But if I were to add something, you'd be in danger of thinking that there's something more to say. But no words can express it! Everything I've just said has nothing at all to do with it. And furthermore, everything ever said about God, enlightenment, eternal life, and so on is utter nonsense and hasn't the least to do with the inexpressible reality. "Why take autumn leaves for gold?"

All religious and philosophical assertions can be likened to an empty fist held out in play to a child. The child believes there's something in it—but there's nothing in it. The truth is not contained in any spiritual system. You can search as long as you like. You can spend your whole life studying all religious and philosophical teachings, but they have nothing to do with the truth. That's why I advise you: Let everything go! Free yourselves of everything! Don't waste your time senselessly. Remember the admonishing words of Buddha: "This world will come to pass and all that is important will fly away. Each of you must

7

awaken from your dream; there is no time to lose." All things are like dreams, visions, blossoming out of nothing. To chase after them—what a futile undertaking.

Just Avoid Picking and Choosing

The highest truth is not difficult,
just avoid picking and choosing.
—Zen Master Seng-ts'an,
seventh century

You're generally accustomed to viewing things as having a specific value in life, as requiring a certain effort to obtain. Then along comes Zen Master Seng-ts'an and says, "The highest truth is not difficult." What do you make of that? "The highest truth" stands for the meaning of your life, the meaning of all being. That's why the Chinese character for Tao also stands for "meaning." The meaning of the entire universe is Tao, and Tao is the "highest truth." But how can we experience and realize this highest truth without the slightest difficulty?

In order to earn even a little money, you have to exert some effort. But attaining the highest thing there is—something of such gigantic proportions that my mouth is not big enough to proclaim it to you—should come without the slightest difficulty? Let me say this: Not only is the highest truth not difficult; it's the *easiest thing in the world!* Nothing could be easier. Only when you set about it the wrong way does it become difficult.

The problem is that even if you exert a great amount of effort, you'll never be able to find what you seek because the object of your search is *ever present,* your most personal possession. Chinese Zen Master Da-zhu (eighth century) says: "The treasure house within you contains everything and you are free to use it. You don't need to seek outside." You are it! What you seek is your own reality. You've never lost it; it's always there. It's just that you've covered it up with the projections of your illusory thoughts. The highest truth you seek is right in front of you; it manifests itself in all forms, in all phenomena.

A monk once came to Chinese Zen Master Tsao-shan (ninth century), the founder of the Tsao-tung school, and asked, "What about phenomena is true?" And Tsao-shan said, "Phenomenon is truth, and truth is phenomenon." The monk went on to ask, "And where is it revealed?" "Here!" said the Master as he held his tea tray in the air.

Everything is reality. Yet you superimpose impressions of multiplicity and separateness over reality. If you were to ask me, "Where is reality revealed?" I would indicate this gong here. But I could just as well point to that lamp or to this picture. All that you perceive, everything is reality—the highest truth.

> *"The highest truth is not difficult,*
> *just avoid picking and choosing."*

"Picking and choosing" would be, for example, if you were to say, "Here I am in beautiful surroundings, sitting by the sea. I hear the sound of the surf, smell the wonderful salt air, hear the cry of the seagulls—fantastic—this is a spiritual dimension." And then on the other hand say, "Now I'm in a sleazy bar with half-naked bar girls, cigarette smoke, the smell of alcohol, and cheap perfume—this is the world of desire and it can't be the truth." That's exactly the picking and choosing that will be your doom.

Everywhere, wherever it may be, is the reality you seek. And if you can't find it in the midst of action and the world of desire, then you won't find it in a wonderful Buddhist temple, or in any other beautiful "sacred" place because that, too, is only another deception with which you fool yourselves. You must transcend both the profane and the sacred. Don't cling to anything!

A monk once asked Master Tsao-shan (the master with the tea tray): "Who wields the sword in this empire?" And Zen Master Tsao-shan said, "I do! I, Tsao-shan wield the sword!" And the monk asked, "Whom do you intend to kill with it?" "Everyone!" said the Master. "But what if you were to encounter your parents, would you kill them too?" "Why should I make an exception?" said the Master. "All right," said the monk, "but then you'd still be left over!" "What's to be done then?" asked the Master. "You could kill yourself!" said the monk. Tsao-shan replied: "I wouldn't know where to begin."

This is complete and utter *nondiscrimination*. Neither accepting nor rejecting. That's why Zen Master Lin-chi often says: "You still haven't left your family!" In other words, you still haven't left your conditionings, patterns of behavior, and modes of thought behind. You continue to be a prisoner of your limited views and fixations, you don't yet abide in the cloudless clarity of the Mind and thus still stand in the shadow of discriminating thought.

In his work *Hsin-hsin-ming*, the Seal of Faith, Zen Master Seng-ts'an further says: "When you no longer love or hate, the truth reveals itself clear and infinite."

When you are free of love and hate, which means of accepting and rejecting, attachment and aversion, the highest truth reveals itself clear and infinite. In other words, it reveals itself

11

when you no longer differentiate or pick and choose. It's essential to remember, however, that this applies to your inner attitude of mind.

Yin and yang belong together and complement one another. You can't have one without the other. It's like trying to run an electric current without the minus pole, through the plus pole alone. Or like wanting the sun to shine every day and never have rain again.

Everything is *one* reality, be it a pretty butterfly, a beautiful flower, or the pile of dog shit you just stepped in on the sidewalk. Why differentiate? Everything is *one,* for everything is an organic, all-encompassing whole, containing everything within itself—nothing can be removed.

There's nothing you can remove from reality, not even a speck of dust. If it were possible for you to remove anything from the universe—be it but a speck of dust—the entire universe would collapse. Even when you disintegrate an atom in a laboratory, you merely change it into another form of energy. You can't destroy, dissolve, or make anything disappear—you can only *change its form.*

That's why everything is one great *tantra,* meaning a great transformation. And your aim is to be harmony with this. The entire universe is in constant motion. Be one with this motion, don't try to go against it—and you will find yourselves in Tao! Simply don't differentiate, and you will see that everything is good, just as it is, and were it not, that, too, would be good. You can experience the world as a wonderful paradise, but you can also experience it as hell. The last time we met I described the encounter between Zen Master Hakuin (eighteenth century) and the samurai who asked him: "Is there a heaven and hell?" And Hakuin said, "Who are you to ask me such a question?" "Can't you see? I'm a samurai of the Imperial Guard!" replied the samurai. Hakuin said, "Impossible. Our emperor would never engage such a wretched-looking character." Upon hearing these words, the samurai drew his sword and charged toward Hakuin, who raised his hand and said with a smile, "The gates to hell have just opened." The samurai stopped short, put away his sword, and bowed to Hakuin. And Hakuin said, "The gates to paradise have just opened."

You alone project this entire world-show or dreamworld, just as you perceive it. And don't forget that all the experiences reported in the *Tibetan Book of the Dead,* for example, are merely projections of consciousness. This holds for all of the wrathful buddhas and all other frightening figures, as well as for the beautiful, peaceful buddhas that appear in the vision of *bardo,* the intermediary state between death and rebirth. They're all no more than projections of consciousness.

Thus it's critical for you to acquire *clarity* and awareness of Mind *during this lifetime.* It's very important that you abide in the awareness of Mind right in the midst of activity, everywhere—regardless, so that in bardo, you can recognize all phenomena as your own projections. For, just as you project phenomena in everyday life, you also project phenomena in bardo. The process is one and the same; there's not the slightest difference. However, upon seeing through all phenomena as your own projections, you'll instantly experience your ascent above the dark haze of phenomena into the clear light of reality.

If you remain separated from reality by even a hair's breadth, you're as far away from it as is heaven from earth. "The smallest is the same as the biggest, and the biggest is the same as the smallest," says Lao-tzu. It's the same here. When you shoot your bow and arrow and miss your target, then you've missed, be it by a centimeter or a meter; it doesn't make any difference.

Don't differentiate, even between life and death! One day a monk came to Zen Master Tsao-shan, whom we heard about earlier, and requested, "Please heal me Master, I am sick." Tsao-shan said, "I will not heal you." "Why not?" asked the monk, to which Tsao-shan replied, "So that you neither live nor die."

Neither live nor die! Ho! [At this instant the Master hits the gong's metal frame with a wooden stick!] Does this Ho belong to life or to death? Whatever you say is wrong. Only once you surpass it does it reveal itself. Then we will stand eye to eye and every word will be superfluous. Accepting and rejecting, right and wrong, good and bad, worldly and spiritual: all is the "struggle between obedience and resistance." The worldly exists only when you distinguish between worldly and spiritual; the spiritual reveals itself only when you cease clinging to the spiritual. This is how the spiritual manifests itself in the world. "Whoever remains separated from this truth by even a hair's breadth is as far apart from it as is heaven from earth." And that's what Zen Master Seng-ts'an calls the "disease of the soul."

[Silence]

When I pause for a while as I just did, some of you may start to think: I wonder what will come next. But I tell you: It's already here! Anything that could possibly come is already here. There's nothing to wait for. The *true word* was spoken long before you were born. When you are here, it is here!

A novice came to Zen Master Hsüan-sha (ninth century) and said, "Master, I'm new at the monastery and I seek the way to enlightenment. Please advise me how to find it." Master Hsüan-sha asked, "Do you hear the rush of the river?" "Yes, Master." "That is the way," said the Master.

And so I ask you: Do you hear the sound of the rain? If so, *that is the way!*

You Lack Nothing

Students of the way, if you wish to become buddha,
you need not study any doctrine; you must only learn to avoid
seeking and attaching yourselves to anything.
—Zen Master Huang-po, ninth century

These few words from Zen Master Huang-po should be enough to bring someone who heard them just once to enlightenment in a flash because they contain all you need. They lack nothing.

This is pure Zen and wonderfully articulated—and yet it's non-sense. "Students of the way, if you wish to become buddha . . ." How can you desire to become something you already are? How can you desire to gain something you already have and have had since eternity as your most inherent being?

And yet what Huang-po says is correct. Because you believe you've lost your true being and need to regain it, he gives you this advice: "Students of the way, if you wish to become buddha,

15

you need not study any doctrine." And thus he remedies your errors. The belief that you must *become* buddha, an enlightened being, is your first error because you already are the true buddha. A second error occurs when you further believe that you must study a philosophy or some other kind of doctrine in order to become enlightened.

It's important that you realize that there is nothing to attain. *Absolutely nothing!* There is no doctrine that needs to be studied. This view is the essential prerequisite for an understanding of Zen.

> *"You must only learn to avoid seeking and attaching yourselves to anything."*

True Zen learning is to learn that there is nothing to learn. The Unborn Mind is present when nothing is sought. It's also present while you seek it, but your seeking is what obscures it! The moment you stop seeking, the reality of your original condition, meaning the original condition of the Mind, will shine forth and illuminate the entire universe with its incomparable radiance. As long as you continue seeking, as long as you are prey to the erroneous assumption of there being something to find, be it even as tiny as a speck of dust, you fall into the realm of duality. You fall into the realm of affirmation and negation, of distinguishing between right and wrong, and are bound ever tighter to the cycle of birth and death. Zen Master Huang-po says: "The indestructible Mind is present where there is no attachment."

The opposite of attachment is to *let go*. It would be logical for you to say: "Okay then, I'll let go." However, this type of letting go is not the letting go of Zen. It doesn't correspond to the attitude of mind of *wu-wei,* nondoing, and *wu-nien,* nonthinking. It's really only a *desire* to let go, an activity of the ego. As such, it causes inner tension, for tension is impeded desire. Therefore, attachment can't be undone by *doing* the opposite, letting go. All opposites, being and nonbeing, life and death, coming and going, right and wrong, belong to the dualistic realm of ignorance. To make this distinction clear, I'd like to tell you about an encounter between a monk and Zen Master Joshu (ninth century).

A monk came to Zen Master Joshu and said, "Look, I've let go of everything. There is nothing left in my consciousness. What do you say to that?" Joshu unexpectedly replied, "Then throw it away!" The monk was astounded and insisted, "But Master, I just told you I've let go of everything. What's left to throw away?" To this Joshu said, "If that's so, you'll have to carry it further."

The letting go you *do* will turn into a letting go that holds you back. You will become prisoners of your "self-made" letting go. The indestructible Mind is present *only* where there is *no* attachment. This is where the clear light of reality dawns.

Countless methods exist as philosophies or religious disciplines, such as performing prostrations or *kundalini* meditation and *yantra* meditation, to name a few. All these artificial methods and doctrines that are supposed to work against delusion amount to no more than hocus-pocus—puffs of air in empty space. There is nothing to be attained and there are no forms of delusion to be destroyed. Even the notion itself that something exists that can be destroyed is delusion.

People often ask me: "What is your teaching?" There is no teaching here because teachings endanger the free mind. All teachings are dangerous because they turn into dogmas. In addition, preoccupation with various doctrines and artificial methods only wastes your spiritual energy. There is nothing to learn, nothing to gain, and nothing to find. Whoever believes that there is something to seek is like a blind person looking for a nonexistent black cat in a pitch-black room.

If suddenly, *all at once*, you realize that your *own Mind* is the divine reality you seek, and that there is nothing to attain, no deed to accomplish—that is the highest realization! It means you have realized the buddha-nature and have yourself become the buddha you have always been at the ground of your being. On the other hand, all of the countless methods that are supposed to bring humanity to the threshold of liberation belong themselves to the realm of delusion. The gate to liberation is always present—*here and now!* It only requires that you be present to experience it. When you are *here now,* the gate to liberation is here, too.

There is nothing more to do. There is no longer any religious practice to carry out, no dharma, no spiritual precept to fulfill; there is nothing left for you to lean on—one of the reasons being that you no longer need support. You can throw your crutches away.

"Take up your bed and walk!" Jesus says to the lame man. The lame man is someone who has lost his reality, forgotten who he is, and is no longer able to free himself from the attractions of the world because of his earth-binding identification with temporal things. He lies on the earth and can't get up. And Jesus says to him: "Rise, take up your bed and walk!" This means relinquishing all delusion; it is total liberation. This is how you rise above all your conditionings, which are the result of your identification with the entwined memories of a dead past.

Once you have the courage to let go of everything and to leave everything as it is, at that moment, the reality of what you really are will shine forth. Once you were lame; now you can walk again. Once you were blind; now your eyes have opened. You will stride across the whole universe, free from birth and death.

Everything Is the One Mind

Buddha and all sentient beings are nothing but the
One Mind, beside which nothing exists.
—Zen Master Huang-po, ninth century

This statement by Chinese Zen Master Huang-po shatters all conventional, rational thinking. With one yank it pulls the floor out from under your feet. All at once everything to which you are accustomed and all that is familiar to you is thrown into question.

We have often used the illustration of soap bubbles in empty space. It serves well for helping to make things a bit clearer: The endless expanse of the heavens is the *one* space, the *sole* reality. Now imagine a multitude of soap bubbles floating around within it.

What we view as external form—the iridescent soap bubbles—are sentient beings. What surrounds the soap bubbles (the endless expanse of the heavens) is no different from what's inside the soap bubbles (the emptiness). Yet the intellect arbitrarily divides the space of the heavens, which stands for the infinite expanse of the Mind, into inner and outer, unity and multiplicity. The multiplicity is, however, no more than a delusion because that which looks so stable in form has no substance of its own.

We can also see the soap bubbles as representing the five *skandhas*. These elements of existence that give rise to the delusion of personality are: corporeality or form, sensation, perception, mental formations, and consciousness. They correspond to the soap bubble's round form, how we see it, its colors, surface tension, and so on. Together these factors produce an apparent whole and the illusion of a separate entity. It has no real being, rather, it is merely an occurrence—a process of mental and physical phenomena. At the instant the soap bubble bursts, when the apparition vanishes, at that moment the boundless expanse of the *one* being—the One Mind—reveals itself.

This One Mind, the reality of your *true being*, is unborn and indestructible. Just as the expanse of outer space is indestructible, so, too, is the inner space of the soap bubble. At the instant when the soap bubble dies—when it bursts—the only thing that disappears is the outer shell. The only thing that dies is the chemical process of an interplay of different factors creating the perceived image of the soap bubble. And this had no being of its own to begin with. Everything that is dependent on something else for its cause, as Buddha's teaching tells us, falls under the law of coming into being and passing away—and thus is transitory.

But what's *inside* is the indestructible center. It's that which gets its being from itself. At the same time this absolute center is the all-encompassing, organic totality that holds everything within it. It's your *true being* and has no beginning or end. That's why when the scribes and Pharisees asked Christ where he came from and who he was, he responded: "I am the Alpha and the Omega," meaning, "I embrace the beginning and the end—I am eternity!"

What has a beginning will also have an end. But what has *no* beginning will have *no* end, because the Mind that has no beginning is unborn and indestructible. It is neither this nor that, for Mind doesn't belong to the category of things that exist or do not exist.

It's beyond all designation in the form of "being or nonbeing." Western philosophy says: "To be or not to be, that is the question!" Chinese Zen Master Yüan-wu (twelfth century) says in *Bi-yän-lu,* the Blue Cliff Record: "Whoever reflects upon being or nonbeing loses life and limb!"

When we say that the One Mind is neither this nor that, it means that it is beyond all duality. If you take a designation, even just one term, and it gives rise to but a single thought, then a second thought is sure to follow. The moment something becomes fixed, its opposite has already arisen on its own. That's why Lao-tzu says: "When someone says the beautiful is beautiful, the ugly is already there! When someone says the good is good, the bad is already there!" Good and bad, yes and no, right and wrong are all manifestations of discriminating conceptual thought—the structure of the ego. This is where the whole dream of a myriad dualistic phenomenal world arises. And you, the dreamers, are caught in your own delusion of a cycle of birth and death.

It's like playing with an endless thread. You pull at it here and there and wrap a little around your finger, hand, and foot; you spin and joyfully waltz about, and before you know it, you've become so completely entangled that you can no longer free yourselves! You've created a net, a *veil of maya,* and have become entangled in it; the more you try using conceptual thought to free yourselves from this self-constructed prison, the longer you remain trapped within it.

21

Yet behind this entire deception is your true self—the *One Mind*. It's like the movie screen on which all projections, images, forms, and movements take place. The Mind itself remains untouched, regardless of what happens.

You tend to view your thoughts—all your projected concepts and notions—as being separate from the one who thinks them. That's a big mistake, a totally wrong point of view! The thinker is, as I've already said, no more than the end effect of the interplay of the five elements of existence, the skandhas, that create the delusion of personality. The thinker is but the sum of his or her thoughts; in other words: He is *thinking itself*. But because he thinks he's something that is behind thoughts and perception, he considers himself to be the center of all he experiences. And that's precisely the process that sustains ego delusion.

There is much discussion today about the necessity of destroying one's ego. You need only go into a bookstore and take a look at the psychology and esoteric books. Everywhere you read: "The ego must be destroyed." This utterly false belief has its roots in a complete lack of understanding. How can you destroy an ego that doesn't even exist? The ego is merely a *process,* a *phenomenon.* That's why the only thing to obliterate or destroy is the *delusionary notion* of an independent ego—of a thinker behind the thoughts.

Now let's return to Huang-po. Elsewhere he says: "That which is before you is the One Mind. Begin to reason about it and you will at once fall into error." How can that which is before us be the One Mind? It's because everything is the One Mind in the form of what we perceive. This gong here, the altar with the Buddha statue, this lamp, everything you see is made of the same reality of the One Mind. It's always here! It's always right before your nose in a variety of appearances, in all possible forms. Mind is not the opposite of matter but, rather, the stuff of matter. It's the substance and thus the sole foundation of all that is material, of all that is form.

Form, however, has no reality of its own. It's what Buddhism calls *shunyata,* meaning "void" or "emptiness." Everything is empty. "Form is emptiness, and emptiness is form," says the *Mahaprajnaparamita Hridaya Sutra,* the Heart Sutra of Transcendent Wisdom. Form is none other than *emptiness,* and emptiness shows itself as *form.* All is one, without a second. But because of your discriminating perception, you divide everything into the perceiver as subject, the perception process, and the perceived as object. And that makes three. But actually these three are *one. All multiplicity is illusion!* There is only a single being, the One Mind, beside which nothing else exists. It's the sole reality at the deepest ground of all living beings and of all things. In truth, neither living beings nor objects exist separate from one another. Accordingly, material existence, including the entire external world of phenomena, is just an illusion, a cognitive by-product. That's why Huang-po says: "Everything is the One Mind, beside which nothing exists."

Everything you can devise or philosophically acquire through rational analysis and conceptual, discriminating thought is mere speculation and has nothing to do with reality. It causes you to fall ever deeper into mental confusion and to distance yourself ever further from the clear light of the Mind that shines behind all of that. This reality that transcends thought is *your true being!* Wake up! Stop dreaming! And the original condition of your being will shine forth and fill the entire universe with its brilliance. This is your true face before your birth.

Enlightenment in a Flash

*If an ordinary man, when he is about to die,
could only see the five elements of existence as void,
he would receive enlightenment in a flash.*
—Zen Master Huang-po, ninth century

This wonderful text by Huang-po goes straight to the heart of Zen. Huang-po makes a point of saying the "ordinary" man to indicate not just someone who is specially chosen or who has special talents, but every human being. It's possible for everyone, regardless of who he or she is, to attain enlightenment.

"If an ordinary man, when he is about to die, could only see the five elements of existence (corporeality, sensation, perception, mental formations, and consciousness) as void . . ." *That's it!* The whole problematic nature of your situation stems from your being accustomed to identifying yourselves with the ancient memories of a dead past. You constantly identify yourselves with old patterns of behavior and modes of thought, believing that's what constitutes your personality. That's why all of you who come to me are very distinguished individuals. Everyone is exceptional.

Everything with which you identify yourselves, all your memories beginning from the first days of your childhood, this entire sum of experiences forms your alleged individuality. This persistent notion further produces, as it hardens into the armor of the ego, the illusion of an independent, self-existing individual, separate from everything he or she perceives and experiences.

I am I and you are you; we are two different things—this is the dualistic view of the average worldly person. I am you and you are I; whoever sees me, sees us; in our self we embrace the universe—this is the viewpoint of the enlightened person. This is the cosmic dimension of the all-encompassing whole. All supposed multiplicity is an organic, self-contained, all-encompassing, all-pervading whole. Pythagoras says: "The whole is greater than the sum of its parts."

The perception of multiplicity is merely the result of dualistic thinking. You divide subject, object, and the process of perception into three different things. Huang-po says: "If an ordinary man, when he is about to die, could only see the [personality forming] elements of existence as *void*," meaning to recognize as "unreal."

"Form is emptiness, and emptiness is form," says the *Mahaprajnaparamita Hridaya Sutra,* the Heart Sutra of Transcendent Wisdom, which is recited daily in Zen monasteries. The skandhas are empty. Corporeality is empty, sensations are empty, perceptions, mental formations, and consciousness are empty. Consequently, sight, hearing, smell, touch, taste, and thinking are empty, too. Empty—that is to say, lacking their own substance, their own being. They're no more than phenomena without the slightest reality.

The entire external phenomenal world has only relative being as does a mirage, for example, the existence or presence of which you can't deny. You can actually see a mirage: a wonderful oasis with a refreshing spring and beautiful plants. You can see it, but it is no more than a phenomenon and thus has only a relative reality. In the same way, the whole world has only relative reality. The world is merely appearance. It appears to be something it's not, for it's nothing but a gigantic delusion.

The entire contents of our awareness is just appearance without real being. But *being itself* is unconditional being, independent of anything that has gone before, and thus having its own being. As the reality of the One Mind, it is the ground of all things, which is why it is just as it is—suchness, *tathata*.

"If an ordinary man, when he is about to die . . ."

The moment of death is decisive. It's the moment in which our accustomed and familiar awareness, the feeling of stability of an external phenomenal world, begins to fade. Everything dissolves away. There's nothing left for us to cling to. The entire past, our whole life is no more than a memory. Everything merges together to a single point. And because no further movement takes place, this dimension becomes increasingly powerful. It's a cutoff, a radical *end!* The thread of life is severed. The pearls of identification on this string of pearls tumble to the ground, roll away, and disappear.

Enlightened masters of all religions have always maintained that the moment of death is crucial, because as Emerson once said, "You will become what you desire." At that moment you will be drawn to that on which your heart dwells. These identifications, whatever they may be, generate the tendencies of the *samskaras,* the karmic formational forces, which determine everything about your earthly existence. Their influence also extends through *bardo*—the interval state between death and rebirth—and thus determines the form your rebirth will take in the next life.

If, however, at the moment of death you realize the emptiness of this whole deception, of this great ruse, all identifications and attachments will melt away on their own. The very instant you perceive the emptiness of all existence, meaning the emptiness of all apparent existence, release will spontaneously occur.

> *"If an ordinary man, when he is about to die, could only see the five elements of existence as void . . ."*

This is what it comes down to. My question to you is Why wait around for the moment of death? Why not die the *mystical death—now!* At this instant! The seventeenth-century mystic Angelus Silesius says: "Die, ere you die, so that when you die, you won't be ruined." And this is our way of Zen practice, the way of *zazen,* the way of dying into the *great death.*

If you let go now while you still have the power to think clearly and decide for yourselves, see through the deception and radically immerse yourselves in *here and now,* then space and time and hence all else will melt away. And the absolute reality behind the whole spectacle, the empty movie screen of the Self-Mind, the original condition of your mind, will shine forth with undiminishing clarity.

Yet the slightest hesitation can result in the loss of life and limb. "Truthful words are not beautiful and beautiful words are not truthful," says Lao-tzu. The deeper and more direct a statement is, getting to the heart of the matter, the less edifying are its words in a general sense. Such statements invariably pull the foundation of your ego's armor out from under it. Everything that gives you alleged security in the time and space dimension of *samsaric* delusion dissolves away.

It's as if you were to find yourself floating about on an ice floe far out in warm waters. The ice floe begins to melt. You can't hold on to it any longer. Even if you try, it will melt nonetheless and return whence it came. You have only two choices: either remain in this deluded state of attachment, which will cause you to drown in fear and horror at the dissolution of the pseudo-foundation of an apparently stable external world, or be in accord with Tao.

When you are in accord with Tao, you move with the flow and don't try to oppose it. Even when everything melts away, you feel no fear or terror for it means the harmonious homecoming to the original condition of your being. When you realize that the personality-forming elements of existence have no being and all you perceive is no more than an illusion, you will achieve a state of inner detachment from everything. This type of detachment, however, has nothing to do with the dualistic attitude of mind of accepting or rejecting, because the ice floe, to return to our example, is no different from the water surrounding it.

Zen Master Hakuin (eighteenth century) says: "People are in essence buddha. It is like water and ice: just as there is no ice without water, there are no people without buddha. Woe be to those who search afar not knowing what lies at hand! They are just like others who cry out in thirst while standing in the midst of water."

Everything is the One Mind. There is nothing which is not the One Mind. It's just that the habitual way in which you see things and situations, in terms of attachment and aversion, causes you to project the delusion of a feared snake over the reality of an ordinary rope.

It's only your imagination, activated by fear, that produces a snake. Your joy, for example, produces a flower. Your imagination can produce anything. It's just like going to a potter. The potter has clay from which he is able to produce a variety of forms. Looking at his display, you see many different-shaped vessels: pitchers, vases, bowls, cups, and so on, a grand assortment of items, an incredible diversity of forms. Yet all these different things are nothing but the same old clay.

The *samskaras* (your karmic formational forces) form the

objects, and the substance (the clay) is the One Mind. So, my friends, why continue to throw pots? Why not abide in the original condition of the Mind? *Free yourselves of everything!* Be what you are without generating any overlay! It's so simple, truly so simple!

The sole cause of your dilemma is that you've forgotten who you are. If you hadn't forgotten, you wouldn't have come here. You've come to ask me who you are. How peculiar!

The wave asks the ocean: "Who am I?" And the ocean answers: "I am you!" All of you are the ocean. You yourselves are the reality you seek. Christ says: "The Father and I are one," which means: Whoever sees me, sees us. There is no difference.

Because of its conceptual fixation, thinking leads to differentiation, which causes the illusion of multiplicity to arise. Where there is multiplicity, there is also separation. You view yourselves apart from the whole and thus give rise to all problems. When thoughts arise, all things arise; when thoughts cease, all things cease, including all problems. Thinking generates karmic forces that activate emotional impulses and mental formations, creating all types of mental images.

It's no different from dreaming when you are asleep at night. There is no need to dream; nonetheless, memories and the undigested impressions of the day begin to act as karmic formational forces. They arise and form themselves into all kinds of situations and circumstances.

Soji Enku often used to say: "When thoughts arise, wisdom ceases." And let me add: "When thoughts disappear, reality dawns." All thoughts must disappear! So if you want to put an end to this nightmare, you must die the mystical death. An ancient Zen master said: "Die and be utterly dead. Then do whatever you want, all is good."

Of course, having someone speak to you of death, of dying and letting go, could lead you to think that this is a gloomy philosophy. But let me tell you, it's not a philosophy, it's the truth.

It seems gloomy only to those who cling to the world. If you cling to it, you'll naturally have a hard time letting go of it. You'll feel just like the child who has built a sand castle and sees someone come along and kick it in. What a pity! But why mistake autumn leaves for gold? Why shed tears over something that has no being anyway?

Whoever resists thinking of death is already spiritually dead. That's why Christ says: "Let the dead bury their own and follow me!" To follow Christ means to accept death and immerse yourself in it completely. In his wonderful poem "The Great Death," Soji Enku says: "The great death, your life, bows over you with a smile. Welcome him with all the roses of love you have ever received."

That's it, that's the truth. The instant you become fully absorbed in death, you will be granted the *great life*. Then you'll jump up and shout: "Ha! Now I know. It's all falsehood and deceit! There is no bondage, there is no liberation, there is no samsara or nirvana. It's all mu! That's how it is. mu, *nothing*!" Become this *nothing*—completely. But don't cling to the word mu, or else you'll be stuck again.

Now! Do you hear it? [The Master holds up a wooden stick.] Now it is present— mu— and mu is *now!* This now is no different from what came before and what will follow, because now is always present. All is now! All is mu!

"Die and be utterly dead. Then do whatever you want, all is good." This dying is to plunge into the great life. The *great death* and the *great life* are one and the same. Letting go completely and being embraced by divine reality is *one* experience. To have it, you need do nothing further than be who you are. In other words: Let your *true face before your birth shine forth!*

The Void Needs No Support

The void needs no support; Mahamudra relies upon nothing.
Without effort, relaxed and natural, you can break the yoke and
achieve liberation. If you see nothing when you look into space
and simultaneously perceive Mind with Mind,
you destroy all discrimination and attain buddhahood.
—Mahamudra Master Tilopa, eleventh century

"The void needs no support;
Mahamudra relies upon nothing."

"Yʘu can't nail a board to the void," says Huang-po. *Mahamudra,* the boundless expanse of the One Mind, needs no support; it relies on nothing. All systems of thought, all the contrived philosophies ever fabricated, such pseudorealities are entirely the consequence of acrobatic cerebral speculation and thus constantly need new crutches, scaffolds, and mental props to keep them from falling in on themselves. But reality itself is inexpressible; it relies on nothing at all.

"Without effort, relaxed and natural, . . ."

There's nothing for you to do, absolutely nothing. It's quite simple. In order to break the yoke and gain liberation without effort, you must be relaxed and natural.

Everywhere you hear that Zen is most difficult, and the majority of Zen books tell you over and over again how very, very hard Zen is. Western interpreters even write that westerners will never be able to fully understand Zen. A huge mystery is made of Zen. But let me tell you: Zen is not difficult; it's *very simple.* I don't say this merely for the sake of argument, but to make clear that the difficulty in understanding Zen lies solely in your not understanding how close you are to the reality you seek. That's the whole secret. And because it's so close that it can't get any closer, there is truly nothing to seek.

That's why we don't practice the bone-breaking Japanese kamikaze form of *zazen,* where all you do is sit on your meditation cushion and stare at the wall. Many Japanese monasteries hold *sesshins* (extended periods of sitting), where all you do is perch on your meditation cushion for days or even weeks and just sit and sit and sit. You're even "generously" allowed to nod off for an hour after midnight on your cushion—provided, of course, you maintain an upright position. Zen Master Lin-chi has the following to say about this type of false practice: "There are certain blind baldies who, after they've eaten their fill, practice zazen. They arrest the movement of their thoughts and to prevent them from even forming, flee the noise of the world and seek silence. This is a deviant form of Zen. It is the pitfall of the dead void."

This dead form of zazen is the exact opposite of the Zen of the ancient Chinese masters. *Zazen* doesn't mean to sit stiff like a corpse. *Za* means "to sit" in the sense of "to abide." *Zen* means "absorption, to be absorbed in reality itself," the source of our being. Hence, *zazen* means "to abide at the source."

32

That's it. Emphasis should not be placed on a physical practice but, rather, on an attitude of mind that is turned inward in everything you do. This is the living Zen of the ancient Chinese masters, and everything else is the abnormal outgrowth of over-strained brains.

"Without effort, relaxed and natural, . . ." This is true zazen and also the attitude of mind of Taoism. We mustn't forget that the ancient Chinese Zen masters such as Hui-neng, Ma-tsu, Pai-chang, Huang-po, Lin-chi, were steeped in the spirit of Tao. The essential element of Taoism is *wu-wei,* nondoing, the relaxed and easeful attitude of mind of nondesire. Tao flows like the water, and when you are in accord with Tao, you flow along with it.

Therefore don't create any barriers or artificial paths! Don't fetter yourselves with dogmatic chains, and don't wall yourselves into the dungeon of any system. Otherwise you will go against the original spirit of Tao and the original spirit of Ch'an (the Chinese word for Zen). And to guard against anyone thinking that here we practice the bone-breaking Japanese form of Zen, we call our center the Tao Ch'an Center!

"Without effort, relaxed and natural, you can break the
yoke and achieve liberation."

"Ha!" one of you could say, "Now I've got him. He just spilled the beans: breaking the yoke is a forceful act." But you would be wrong! It's not forceful. The moment you effortlessly abide in a relaxed and natural state, ego fixation and artificial behavior cease. All that remains is the spirit of *wu-wei,* non-doing, and *wu-nien,* nonthinking. That's the true spirit of Zen. And in this state of the cheerful reflection of the Mind, your attachment and identification, desire, hate, and ignorance fade away. The same goes for old age, despair, sickness, pain, and death; they all disappear.

Not that you'll never grow any older or never become sick

again, but these things will come quite naturally, just happen. A plant grows; a bud appears and becomes a flower, blooming in full splendor. It gives out its wonderful scent, attracting bees and butterflies, until the time comes when it loses its petals and falls apart. Everything happens quite naturally, in harmony with Tao.

> *"If you see nothing when you look into space and simultaneously perceive Mind with Mind, you destroy all discrimination and attain buddhahood."*

"If you see nothing when you look into space . . ." This means that when you look into space while abiding in the cheerful reflection of the Mind, things are still apparent, but you no longer see the world in terms of distinguishing between subject and object. You are no longer an egocentric subject perceiving external objects in the discriminating light of right and wrong, of attachment and aversion. Instead, everything is an all-encompassing organic whole in which all is included in a wonderful and perfect manner.

You look outward. But because your perception is no longer dualistic, your outward looking is *non-outward-looking*. There is neither outside nor inside in this state. All that remains is "suchness," *tathata*. Everything is just as it is. All is *one*. The seer, the seen, and the process of seeing are one. The thinker, the thought, and the process of thinking fall together into one and multiplicity melts away.

Neither the object of perception nor the perceiver or thinker has any reality of its own. Everything is merely occurrence! It's all just a psychic process! There is no thinker as subject. The only thing that exists is a sequence of thoughts. My saying that a thinker as subject doesn't exist raises fear in many people. But such fears are totally ungrounded and merely betray attachment to something that doesn't exist. The instant you allow yourselves to become completely immersed in *suchness,* in *here and now,* the phantasm will disappear and there will be no more differentiation. Everything is good just as it is. At that point the reality behind the phenomena, just like the movie screen behind the moving pictures, will reveal itself. The projections of an external multitudinous phenomenal world, caused by the process of attachment and aversion, will be extinguished. The film is over, and the clear light of reality shines forth.

"*. . . and simultaneously perceive Mind with Mind . . .*"

So Tilopa continues. At this moment "the eye with which I see God is the same eye with which God sees me; my eye and God's eye are one eye, one knowing, and one loving," as Meister Eckhart says. This is how "you destroy all discrimination and attain buddhahood." However, attainment can't be compared to climbing a mountain, for example. Nor can it be likened to the eventual achievement of some distant goal. Instead, it's always present.

Christ says: "The kingdom of God is within you," as translated by Luther. Other translations read: "The kingdom of God is among you." Yet the two translations do not contradict each other (contrary to what theologians think); rather, they enhance each other. The reality of all-encompassing being, the reality of the Universal Mind is within you and simultaneously is the reality beneath your very feet. The Chinese Zen masters said: "Look beneath the soles of your feet, there you will find Tao, there you will find nirvana."

*"The clouds that cross the sky do not take root
anywhere, they have no abode, much less do the
discriminating thoughts that cross the mind. As soon as
the Self-Mind is seen, all discrimination ends."*

35

The thoughts and visions that pass through your mind have no reality, no stability; they simply come and go. Just like the clouds that pass before the moon, clouds of thoughts pass before the Self-Mind. There might even be an evening when you look up to a cloudy sky and seeing no moon say: "There is no moon tonight." But yes! The moon is always there, just as is the self-illuminating Self-Mind. It always shines; it's always present. And as soon as the Self-Mind is seen, all discrimination ends. You awaken from your dream of a three-dimensional world of space and time and are free.

There Is Nothing to Seek

*Our original buddha-nature is, in highest truth, devoid of any
atom of objectivity. It is void, omnipresent, silent, and pure. It
is glorious and mysterious peaceful joy—and that is all.*
— Zen Master Huang-po, ninth century

Our original buddha-nature, meaning our true being, the
true original condition of our Mind as seen from the
standpoint of the highest truth, is devoid of any per-
ceptible attribute. It eludes all denomination. It is the being in
which all is contained.

"It is void, omnipresent, silent, and pure."

Our buddha-nature is void *(shunyata)* in the sense that it is
free of all conceptual fixation and has no content. It is the fullness of divine nothing, the beyond-being nonbeing.

It is omnipresent, silent, and pure. And because it is omnipresent, there is no need to seek it. All seeking is brought on by ignorance. You seek under the mistaken assumption that absolute reality can be attained only through the pursuit of various activities. Strive as hard as you like, you will not be able to attain it. The more you strive, the more you distance yourselves from it. This is the great dilemma. All religions and philosophies say you need do this and that, practice asceticism, study philosophical works and commentary, practice *yantra* and *kundalini* meditation, and so on. Zen, on the other hand, simply points—directly and immediately—to the original condition of your being.

The reality you seek reveals itself when you realize that there is absolutely nothing to seek. All seeking is ignorance. You cannot obtain your true being, you cannot seek it. You can, however, be silent and abide in yourself, thus allowing yourself to be found by the almighty essential nature of the One Mind.

We've all heard the parable about the man who tried to force open the gate to paradise. He knocked, kicked, and pushed against it with all his might, but nothing happened. He continued his attempts throughout the night until at last he collapsed to the ground in exhaustion. Finally realizing all his efforts were in vain, he watched with amazement as the gate opened toward him, not away from him as he had supposed it would. That's it! All your striving only pushes shut the gate to liberation.

"There is nothing to gain," is *the* quintessential statement of Zen. There is nothing to attain. The longer you live with the illusion that there is something to attain and something to gain, the more you further yourselves from the original condition of your being, the original condition of the Mind.

What is it you hope to gain? There are no new possessions to acquire. Everything is present *here* and *now!* What good would gaining an inch of land do you when you're already standing smack-dab in the middle of it? Where would you seek? The ancient Chinese said: "If you seek Tao, then look beneath the soles of your feet!"

Once more I'd like to call attention to the passage in the Bible where the Pharisees ask Jesus, "You talk about the kingdom of God. You say it is near and it will soon come. But *how* will we recognize it and *when* will it come?" And Jesus replies: "You will not be able to recognize the coming of the kingdom of God by external signs. Nor will you be able to say, 'Look, here it is!'or 'See there!' For the kingdom of God *is within you.*" This is Martin Luther's translation. Other translations read: "The kingdom of God *is among you.*" Biblical scholars and theologians disagree and argue about which is the correct translation, *"within you"* "or *"among you."* But actually both are correct. One complements the other.

"The kingdom of God is *within* you" means that God's kingdom is the core of everything. It's your innermost self, the place and origin of all life. It's the "cave of divine darkness," the "*krypta* of the heart," as the Christian mystics say. This is where the light of your true nature shines. Your *innermost self* is the kingdom of God "within you." And this innermost self is *now!*

The innermost self is never the past nor the future. Such are merely clouds that pass in front of the clear light of the Mind and have no substance. Behind them shines reality with undiminishing clarity—eternal, unborn, indestructible, beyond the bounds of space and time, eternally being itself. It manifests itself as the foundation of all you experience and thus is "among you."

If you seek Tao, you'll find it right where you are; you're standing on it. Look beneath the soles of your feet! It's here and nowhere else, which means it's *everywhere!* Wherever you go, wherever you stand, wherever you are, the unchanging buddha-essence, the source of the entire cosmos, is present. Why go crazy chasing around the globe looking for something you've never lost? What a delusion. It's *always present.*

"It is void," says Huang-po, "omnipresent, silent, and pure."
Void means that everything that you experience within the space
and time dimension of your worldly perception lacks its own
reality. Nothing in the world of experience gets its being from
itself. Yet the reality *behind* all experience is the reality that is
the foundation of everything. It eludes all conceptualization in
terms of being or nonbeing, substance or nonsubstance. As such
it is "void" (shunyata).

> *"It is glorious and mysterious peaceful joy—*
> *and that is all."*

How will you be able to find this true joy? You'll find it only
when you immerse yourself in the original condition of your
Self-Being, in the original condition of the Mind. Your true self
is none other than glorious and mysterious peaceful joy.

But if you go about with the cramped demeanor of a pall-
bearer, convinced of being able to obtain great joy through
conceptual thought and the moral attitudes of acceptance and
rejection, of right and wrong, you're on the wrong track. As
long as you remain attached to duality and maintain the belief
of thus being able to gain access to mysterious peaceful joy, to
experience great divine joy—forget it. If you do not open
yourself to this joy, you will never experience true joy. On the
contrary, divine joy will take to its heels upon catching sight
of you.

I have often said: As long as you do not dwell in inner joy
and truly breathe the joy of being, totally experience and feel it
in every pore of your body, you will remain caught in illusion.
And by joy, I don't mean the external type you feel only when
things are going your way, when, for example, you find yourself
in bed with your lover or surrounded by a beautiful landscape,
or when you are seated before a good meal and say: "Oh, how
marvelous. I feel great, fantastic—what a wonderful world!"

Wrong! Joy is *everywhere,* regardless of where you are! In other words, it's not something you can produce.

Joy is there once you let go of all you consider important, what you believe you are, and what you think belongs to you. But this kind of letting go is not a matter of self-will, for if *you want* to let go, you'll wind up hanging on to letting go. Then before you know it, letting go is hanging on to you. Just leave everything as it is, and the joy behind everything will reveal itself.

Leave everything, regardless of what it is, as it is. Don't project your moral attitudes, conceptual fixations, patterns of behavior, and conditionings over your awareness of things. Instead, let everything take its natural course. Simply go with the flow! You walk through town and pass a pretty woman who smiles at you. It is good. Then you come across a babbling drunk who swears at you. It is good. Everything is good just as it is, for all is one ocean of being. One wave is somewhat rounder, the other a bit pointier, another has a foam crest, and another more bubbles. Yet everything is the one ocean. Everything is perfect.

Be one with Tao, don't fixate, don't label, don't judge. Abide in the original condition of the Mind. Wake up! Stop your dreaming! And that means *tathata* (suchness). That's why Buddha is called the *tathagata,* the "thus-come one," the one who is perfectly enlightened.

To awaken is to be free of all conditioning. It's not things you become free of, but, rather, you become free of the false way in which you view things. If you continue your attempts to free yourself of things and of your attachment to things, you'll only go in circles like a dog trying to bite itself in its stump of a tail. Round and round the dog goes, without success.

Now then, you can't produce it. Zen is a radical break in the whole of your so-called spiritual life, which is not a true spiritual life at all, even though most people would consider it as

41

such. Your efforts take on many forms: meditation, study of texts, and so on. That's all fine and good. Zen, on the other hand, takes the sword of realization and slices through the Gordian knot of your spiritual confusion. The entire delusionary structure falls to pieces, and the endless expanse of the One Mind bursts forth.

Indeed, this is what makes Zen different. If there's a tree that needs removing, Zen doesn't start by snipping the itty-bitty leaves one by one from the top of the tree, moving on to clip the tiny branches, and so on and so forth until the bottom is reached. Even before getting to the bottom of the tree, new growth begins shooting at the top, and thus the whole process starts all over again. That's not the way of Zen. Zen raises the sword of realization and cuts down the whole tree with one stroke. Whack! The whole delusionary structure is cut to the roots. That's it.

This is what the true way comes down to, which is why it's the sole way I have to offer. It's the way of total liberation. In the words of Huang-po: "Mind is filled with radiant clarity, so cast away the darkness of your old concepts. Free yourselves of everything!" Now you may be thinking: "Where do I begin with total liberation? Maybe I should start with my car. I really don't need such a large vehicle. A small one would do just as well." And off you go to tackle one thing after the other. But that's precisely the erroneous principle I just finished talking about.

That's no different from trying to fell a tree by beginning with the tiny leaf at the very top. The only real way you can get rid of the problem is to get rid of *yourselves,* which means to eliminate the causing factor. And the causing factor is the ego, the end-product of the three *kleshas,* the three basic errors: *greed, hate,* and *blindness,* which stand for desire, aggression, and ignorance. The three kleshas interact to create the illusion of an independent personality, which amounts to no more than hocus-pocus, lacking any reality whatsoever.

How long do you plan to play this game? Why not awaken?—*now!* At this moment the opportunity is at hand. There's no other time and no better time than *now!* Why wait around? Why say: "The Master gave another good talk today. I think I'm starting to catch on. Some things seem a bit clearer to me, and maybe someday . . ." *Forget someday!* There is no someday. There is only *now!* Besides that, there is nothing. Therefore, enter deeply into it, into the *true being* of the original condition of your Mind. Enter deeply into it by awakening to it yourself.

There is no other path. There is no other way than for you to awaken to your true self. *Awaken!* Quit dreaming and playing around in the sandbox of your conditionings. Cease viewing things through the template of your conceptual fixations, your social ideals and moral attitudes, and judging what is good and what is not good, what is right and what is wrong! There will be no end if you continue in this manner. Therefore, leave everything as it is!

This is a tremendous challenge. Zen calls upon you to leave everything as it is. And to this end there's nothing for you to do. The whole point is not *to do*, but rather *to leave be*. That's it. Let everything go, and the reality of your true being will manifest itself. That which is before you each instant is the One boundless Mind in all its perfection. There is nothing besides it. This Mind, which has no beginning, is unborn and indestructible.

Everything without exception—all living beings, all things— is this buddha-essence in the manifestation of a manifold world. Everything is the One Mind. Yet ignorance, your spiritual blindness, produces waves of thought on the pure reality of the One Mind. These waves are the amazing diversity of forms in an apparent external phenomenal world that you take for reality. Thus you fail to realize that the world you perceive is your own projection, caused and conditioned by desire, hate, and ignorance.

Indeed, absolutely everything you encounter is in truth the One Mind in all its perfection. There is nothing besides it! It includes the pretty woman who passes you on the street and smiles suggestively. It includes the babbling drunk who insults you as you walk by. *Everything* is the flawless, all-encompassing whole of divine being.

And everything you perceive as imperfect is simply your own projection. You project your values, plopping them on top of the object of your perception and taking them for the object itself. But that's a mistake. For as long as you live in the dream of samsara, in the dream of maya, all you perceive is you own projection—just appearance, not being. Being is that which gets its being from itself—it has no beginning or end. Birth, old age, despair, sickness, pain, and death do not exist. There is only the *nonexpressible,* "mu!" and that's it. All else is your own projection.

The nonexpressible is your original face before your birth; it's always present. Even when you go through all the stages of spiritual development to enlightenment; when in a single instant you finally attain perfect realization, you'll only experience the original self that was with you all the time.

My speaking of the many stages of development one goes through one by one on the way to enlightenment is very conceptual and intellectual and totally opposed to Zen. In Zen there are no stages through which to advance to enlightenment. Such are merely wild notions. There is no awakening by stages. There is only a radical here-and-now self-dissolution and self-immersion in the original condition of the Mind.

When you attain perfect realization, you'll experience only the omnipresent buddha-essence that was with you all the time without interruption. That which has always been the foundation of your experience—the perceiver behind all experiences—was always there, but you were always somewhere else. As Meister Eckhart says: "God is within, but you are without."

In this dimension of consciousness, with crystal-clear awareness you'll realize that all you thought you had achieved on your spiritual path up to this point was no more than *empty shells*. You fooled around with empty shells but didn't experience the essence of it all; you didn't come any closer to the heart of the matter.

Do whatever you like: Master all the different philosophies and tackle all of Zen's texts, koans, and mondos. Study and memorize all the sacred scriptures, and scrutinize all of the corresponding commentary. The moment you awaken you'll realize all of this is merely chaff of no value. It's all empty appearance and hasn't the least to do with reality as it really is. Absolutely nothing!

So what are you waiting for? Why continue to come and go so that each time you appear here I'm forced to ask, "Who dragged this body here again for you today?" This entire lifeless accumulation of woven-together memories, behavioral patterns, modes of thought, moral codes, social norms, and so on and so forth, let it all go and let the ever-present reality shine forth and enlighten the entire universe with its divine light.

Beyond All Words

MU MU MU MU MU
MU MU MU MU MU
MU MU MU MU MU
MU MU MU MU MU
—Zen Master Mumon,
thirteenth century

This marvelous poem by the thirteenth-century Chinese Zen Master Mumon was written in a meter of five Chinese characters. It is a profound statement of Zen. Zen Master Mumon could have written *mu* just once. That instead he wrote *mu* in a meter of five characters was no Zennistic joke. His aim was to burn mu as the blazing seal of the buddha-mind into our hearts. Mu! Mu! Be absolutely dead! An ancient Zen master said, "Die and be utterly dead. Then do whatever you want; all is good."

There is another Zen poem by Zen Master Mumon that wonderfully expresses the totality of his enlightenment experience:

A thunderclap in a clear blue sky!
All earthly creatures
Have opened their eyes.
Everything beneath the sun
Has bowed at once.
Mount Sumeru
Jumps up and dances.

"A thunderclap in a clear blue sky!"

The clear blue sky is the clear and empty condition of Mind. When your mind is empty, void of thoughts and concepts, then your true face before your birth will reveal itself. The thunderclap in a clear blue sky is the thunder of silence that rocks the entire universe. The eye of enlightenment is opened with a single clap and you see reality as it really is.

"Mount Sumeru jumps up and dances."

"Huh?" Mount Sumeru dances? What does that mean? Buddhists speak of Mount Sumeru as the center of the universe. And I say that this center is also the core of being and thus the all-encompassing whole in which everything is contained. Mount Sumeru is everything; it is totality itself.

Old age, despair, sickness, pain, and death; coming and going, diversity and unity, everything—the entire dream of being and nonbeing vanishes and Mount Sumeru jumps up and . . . [The Master springs up from his seat and dances.]

Why am I doing this? Because I am Mount Sumeru. You too are Mount Sumeru! There is no other Mount Sumeru, for nothing exists besides your true self. The moment you awaken there is nothing besides this original face before your birth.

*"All earthly creatures
Have opened their eyes.
Everything beneath the sun
Has bowed at once."*

This corresponds to the revelation contained in the bodhisattva vow recited daily in Buddhist monasteries: "I vow to forgo my own liberation until all creatures have been liberated." Many Buddhists cling to the vow, taking its meaning literally and believing this interpretation to be true bodhisattva consciousness. Their understanding is very materialistic. If you had to wait out the entire evolutionary development of all microorganisms, of the smallest living being until it ripens into a human and achieves liberation, then your aspiration for enlightenment would be no more than a wishful dream. You'd wind up trapped forever in the cycle of birth and death, in the dream of a world of multiplicity. You'd never awaken and gain liberation.

In truth, "the whole is greater than the sum of its parts," as Pythagoras says. All is one, and one is all. In the words of the *Lankavatara Sutra:* "Buddha loves all living beings because there are no living beings."

Let's return once more to the enlightenment gata of Zen Master Mumon.

*"All earthly creatures
Have opened their eyes.
Everything beneath the sun
Has bowed at once."*

"All earthly creatures have opened their eyes"—their eyes are open if your eye is open. That's why Meister Eckhart says, "The eye with which I see God and the eye with which God sees me is one eye. It is *one* seeing, *one* knowing, and *one* loving!" No longer is there another eye, another seeing. All that remains is *one* seeing. All earthly creatures have opened their eyes—*all are liberated.* The seer, the seeing, and that which is seen are one. I am you, and you are I. Whoever sees me, sees us. In our Self we embrace the universe.

"Everything beneath the sun has bowed at once." Everything is one, and one is everything. There is no multiplicity and thus no coming or going—no past, no present, and no future. Nothing! There is only an infinite, all-encompassing, boundless joy of being that as such is an *above-being divine nonbeing,* beyond the capacity of conceptual denomination.

This is your original face before birth. Anything I could say about it would fall short of the essential. And now! [The Master holds his staff in the air and remains silent.] Do you hear it? Just now, that was the *true word.* "The thunder of silence!" If you were really able to hear it, the word that speaks in the ground of your being, in the absolute center of here and now, then I could keep silent.

In an old Chinese monastery of the Tang dynasty, the monks despaired. It had been weeks since the last dharma lecture. The Master cloaked himself in silence. The monks grew anxious and started to talk. Finally the elder monks gathered and went to the Master's room. "Master, all the monks in the monastery are worried." "Why? What's the problem?" "You've stopped giving lectures. They want you to teach again. They yearn to hear a good dharma lecture." "Well if that's all it is, then sound the bell! Summon everyone to dharma hall."

The bell sounded. There was shouting and running, and everyone stormed into the dharma hall. They eagerly waited for the Master to make his entrance. Finally the time came. The Master entered the hall, stepped up to the dharma pulpit, and said: "Dear monks, dear assembly. There are learned philosophers who write thick volumes about Buddhism and Zen. Then there are commentators who compose long commentaries about these writings. And then there are so-called teachers who comment on these commentaries. But I am a Zen master, and I ask you to please bear this in mind!" With these words the Master turned and left the hall.

What a fantastic dharma lecture! First-rate! Impossible to top. At our last meeting we heard about Chinese Zen Master Huang-po. On one occasion news traveled throughout the land that the great master planned to deliver an important dharma sermon and that all monks from neighboring monasteries were invited to attend. They came from everywhere, by boat and raft, by donkey, horse, and on foot. Many, of course, rode cows and oxen, an important observation! An essential ascertainment! They rode cows. Perhaps one day you will understand the reason why I value cows so highly. Those who understand the relationship between the cow and Zen . . . But let's stick to the point. Whenever I get started on cowology, I'm in danger of straying from the subject.

So the news spread throughout the land, and people came from everywhere. The dharma hall was hardly big enough to accommodate the crowd of listeners that had gathered.

The big moment came. The bells sounded and the Master stepped up to the lectern and said: "Having many sorts of knowledge cannot compare with giving up seeking for anything, which is the best of all things! Mind is not of several kinds and there is no doctrine which can be put into words. As there is no more to be said, the assembly is dismissed!"

Having thus spoken, Huang-po stepped down from the lectern and left the dharma hall.

So my dear friends, anything I could say would fall short of the essential. And since there is no more to say, today's assembly is dismissed.

Forget Yourself

I have nothing special to say today, not a word. For if I were to say even *one* word, you'd be in danger of clinging to it. You'd look at the word, define it, and relate it to your previous experience. You'd filter it through the screen of your old conditionings, behavioral patterns, and modes of thought; in other words, through all the woven-together memories of a dead past with which you identify yourselves. What comes out at the end has no relation to what I said. That's why it's better for me to remain silent.

[Short silence]

But regardless of the danger I'll say a word. I could pick any word, for example, *mu*! In Zen *mu* means *nothing*. Yet already you are clinging to *nothing*.

Each word causes your thoughts to arise. And "when thoughts arise, all things arise," as Huang-po says. He also says: "When thoughts disappear, all things disappear." One word, one thought, and problems arise, bringing a multitude of emotions with them; and when emotions arise, wisdom ceases. This is how you create your own dualistic world of multiplicity. You find yourselves in a world of joy or a world of suffering, in a world of conflict or in a world of peace depending on what you yourselves create. To illustrate this better I'd like to tell you a little story about a true occurrence: the encounter between Japanese Zen Master Hakuin (eighteenth century) and a samurai.

Armed to the teeth, as was typical in Japan in days of old, a samurai came to Zen Master Hakuin and said: "Master, I'd like to ask you a question." "All right," said Master Hakuin, "go ahead!" The samurai continued, "I'd like to know if there really is such a thing as paradise and hell." Hakuin eyed the samurai from head to toe, made a wry face, and commented, "Who are you to simply come here and ask me such a question anyway?" "Can't you see that I'm a samurai of the Imperial Guard?!" "Hah," said Hakuin. "Impossible! Our emperor would never engage such a wretched-looking character." "What did you say?" cried the samurai (in those days one could do nothing worse than offend a samurai). He drew his sword, held it high over his head, and charged at Hakuin. Hakuin raised his hand, smiled, and calmly said: "The gates to hell have just opened." The samurai stopped short, lowered his sword, and returned it slowly to its sheath. He made a deep bow before the Master. Hakuin then said: "The gates to paradise have just opened."

So you see, this is the precise situation in which you find yourselves—in your self-made world of hell and paradise. Over and over again the experience repeats itself: You feel good, you are satisfied, you lack nothing. Suddenly for no reason a memory surfaces from which you are unable to free yourselves. Thought associations start to arise that lead to a series of emotional impulses, and before you know it, you are depressed or full of aggression. You are in your self-created hell. Yet externally nothing has changed; it all occurs solely within yourselves. You project your own world.

Huang-po says: "The true buddha-essence is mysterious peaceful joy and no more." And this is your *true nature.* In *Viveka-Chudamani,* The Jewel of Discrimination, ninth-century Indian sage Shankara writes: "You are Brahman, pure consciousness, the observer of all experiences! Your true being is joy!" And in the Upanishads, Hinduism's sacred scriptures, we read: "Brahman, divine reality, is *sat-chit-ananda,"* absolute being, absolute consciousness, absolute bliss.

Being, consciousness, and bliss (joy) are your true being. All the rest, meaning all the deluded thoughts you project out of desire and fear, is overlay. Here's an example: A rope is lying across a path in the woods. In the evening you walk along the path, and in the moonlight you think you see a snake. Your fear projects a snake onto the rope lying on the ground. In the same way samskaras, your karmic formational forces, continuously project the illusion of an external world with an endless array of appearances and events. Everything is merely your own projection, because nothing exists besides the reality of the *One Mind.* This reality is ever present and is absolute *now!!!* [The Master strikes a pair of wooden sticks together.]

[Short silence]

As you just heard, this *now* is also *here!* The sound of my striking these two sticks together is not over there or yonder. At the moment you hear the crack, you can't be over there or yonder. That's it. That's the "thunderclap in a clear blue sky," as

Zen Master Mumon says. It's the thunder of silence, Manjushri's sword that with one stroke cuts to pieces the chaos of your delusions.

The cause of all your problems has nothing at all to do with an adverse external world or its imperfect nature. Whatever happens to you, whatever you encounter is your own doing; it's your own projection and nothing further. That's why the three-dimensional world you experience during the day is not the least bit different from the world you experience at night when you dream. Everything you experience in this "world-dream"—the backdrop, the landscape, the living beings, all the problems, the joy and suffering, the coming and going, birth and death, everything, regardless of what it is—is your own projection.

Here and now! That is reality, the true face before your birth, your true being, the reality of the *One Mind.* The One Mind, however, is the *Non-Mind!* Non-Mind stands for the *true empty Mind.* The true empty Mind abides beyond thought and is none other than *shunyata,* emptiness!

In the *Mahaprajnaparamiita Hridaya Sutra,* the Heart Sutra of Transcendent Wisdom, which is recited daily in Zen monasteries, it says: "Form is emptiness and emptiness is form." *Form* refers to everything you perceive. Everything—whether round or square, big or small, colored, black or white—all that constitutes the content of your experience is empty. *Empty* means lacking its own substance, having no being of its own.

The same applies to the six senses: sight, hearing, smell, touch, taste, and thinking. They're all *empty.* Consequently, the product of their interplay is no more than an illusion having no reality whatsoever. If a causing factor lacks reality, then that which the factor causes, the end effect, lacks reality as well.

Hence, the problem of your imprisonment in a three-dimensional world can never be resolved by untying any single small knot of the Gordian knot of your spiritual confusion that you have tied so carefully over the course of untold incarnations.

There is only one solution: Take the sword of *Manjushri*, the bodhisattva of wisdom, and cut the Gordian knot to pieces with one stroke. One stroke, and your hundred thousand problems and troubles, all your delusions fall apart. There is no longer anyone who suffers, and no one who causes suffering. And if no one causes suffering, there can be no one who suffers. If you don't project someone who attacks you, who assaults and threatens you, there is no enemy for you to fight.

We're all familiar with Don Quixote, the dusty old knight who suddenly felt called upon to free the world from evil. He set out on his mission, and wherever he went he saw enemies. Take the windmills for instance. Believing them to be evil giants, he charged at them with his lance and fought until he wound up on the ground half-dead, his clothing torn to shreds.

You constantly battle your own projections. Just as you either fight or flee self-projected images when you dream, you do the same in samsara, the cycle of birth and death. The entire external world you experience has no independent reality; instead it's merely your own projection. Samsara is a cyclical motion; it's the cycle of birth, old age, despair, illness, pain, and death. That's why Buddhism speaks of the *bhava-chakra,* the wheel of life. This wheel of *pratitya-samutpada,* conditioned arising, is depicted in Buddhist iconography. At the hub of the wheel are the three kleshas: desire, hate, and ignorance. As the "three basic evils," they are the driving force behind the entire hocus-pocus conjured up by human consciousness. The kleshas are shown as a a rooster, a snake, and a pig. The rooster stands for desire, the snake for hate, and the pig that roots around in the mud, for ignorance.

Ignorance causes you to project all sorts of impressions, to which you react with acceptance or rejection. When something stands in the way of your self-projected object of desire, you react to this disturbing factor with aggression. This is how desire is brought forth and transformed into hate by spiritual blindness (ignorance). And thus the wheel of life, the *bhava-chakra*, continues to turn because of the driving force of the three kleshas.

You can't escape this situation by solving particular problems or by thinking you can examine your past through psychotherapy and use the results to explain your present situation. Anything you could analyze is a dream occurrence, as is the process of analysis itself.

The only way to obtain liberation is to die out of your self-made prison of ego-armor. "Die, ere you die, so that if you should die, you will not die," says Christian mystic Angelus Silesius (seventeenth century). And twelfth-century Islamic mystic Al Ghazali tells us: "At night you must plunge into the depths of your nothing should a morning dawn for you in the brilliance of the highest light." This is the path to liberation. To die means to *awaken* out of the ego-engendered dream of samsara. Become absolutely nothing—mu!—and you awaken. This is surpassing life and death and thereby surmounting all duality, accepting and rejecting, right or wrong. Die and be utterly dead, and then do whatever you want—all is good.

"Your true being is mysterious peaceful joy and that is all," says Huang-po. Fantastic, wonderful! What is there to complain about? What is there to cry about? After whom or what are you dream dancers chasing? Right now in the silence between my words, if you don't project anything, you can perceive it, your *true divine self,* which illuminates the whole universe with its light. *Forget yourself! Now!* This instant! And enlightenment is there.

Because you've become so accustomed to the dream you project, you've become convinced of the impossibility of awakening to your true being. You come and listen to what I have to say and think, "It sure sounds good; if only I could experience it." Yet in the process you completely forget that all I do is to hold up a large mirror that constantly reflects the reality of your Self-Being.

I never let myself become involved in your ego-games, even when time after time you attempt to lure me into your dream-world. Yet for your own good I sometimes appear to go with you into your dream. At the point when we are dreaming together so pleasantly, I suddenly shout "Ho!" [The Master slams the end of his staff down on a side table.] This then is a great opportunity for you to awaken out of your dream. You are inside the dream and you are caught. On the other hand, I can play with the dream because I'm not caught inside. And what's more, as Master I do not even exist! The master you perceive is simply the reflection of your *true self*. As the "light in the dark-ness," divine grace shows itself to you through the veil of maya.

Had you not left the state of your original being, but, rather, remained within yourselves, you wouldn't be in the situation of coming to me today with the hope that I will reveal the truth to you. And the truth is: Today is the 23rd, tomorrow is the 24th, and yesterday was the 22nd. This has no significance, and there-fore I say: "Ho!!!" Another great opportunity! My dear friends, I mean very well by you. Far better than you could mean with yourselves. For I'm not deceived by your identification with all you believe yourselves to be. I look directly into your hearts and see the true buddha, the perfectly enlightened one. *Tat tvam asi.* That you are. You are I, and I am you; in our self we embrace the universe. Whoever sees me, sees us. Everything is one; there is no multiplicity.

Never forget that all your daily internal and external hard-ships are your own projections without the slightest reality! Here's some advice: Always abide within yourselves. When you abide within yourselves, in the awareness of Mind, what can endanger you considering that there is no multiplicity? And who could threaten and harm you considering that there are no living beings that are separate from one another? That's why the *Lankavatara Sutra* says: "Buddha loves all living beings because there are no living beings." There truly is only the one all-encompassing organic whole, this *one* and nothing besides.

Take Manjushri's sword and cut everything to bits! *Free yourselves of everything!* Whether it be Buddha, Christ, your parents, your children, the whole world, whatever: Take the sword of realization and slay it all, and the dream of samsara, the cycle of birth and death, is over. You awaken, the light of the One Mind shines forth, and *in a flash* you experience that everything is just as it is—*tathata,* "suchness."

Not since the universe came into existence has even a single speck of dust moved. "Mu!!!"

Be Here Now

The One Mind alone is buddha and there is no difference between buddha and sentient beings.
—Zen Master Huang-po, ninth century

"The One Mind alone is buddha." The One Mind and the reality of your Self-Mind is *one and the same reality.* Only a few believe that their own mind is buddha, the absolute. Most Zen students fail to take this seriously and thus live cramped and compulsive lives. But if you are empty and abide effortlessly in awareness of Mind, then you are in a state of natural clarity and attain all-encompassing consciousness. This is the state of nondiscrimination.

The sole cause of discrimination is the whirlwind of thoughts, notions, and concepts; of feelings and conditionings that take the form of behavioral patterns and modes of thought. These work together to produce a thick coating around the core of your Self-Mind. This delusion solidifies into an illusion of form, space, and time that you mistake for your individuality and the world that you experience. You float about like a soap bubble, believing the bubble to be your real being.

Analyze as much as you like. Analyze the soap bubble structure, the surface tension, and the pretty flow of colors. Undergo therapy, study philosophy, but when all is said and done, it will have had no effect on the substance of the soap bubble—*none whatsoever!*

Therefore [the Master hits the side table with his staff], "Die and be utterly dead. Then do whatever you want; all is good." The soap bubble will burst if you are filled with great trust in the divine and have the courage to leave everything as it is, thus yielding yourself through mystical death to the abyss of the divine void. The instant the soap bubble bursts, you will experience yourself in the boundless expanse of the Mind—*your unborn and undying true essence.* You will illuminate and fill the entire universe with the brilliance of the divine light that you *yourself* are.

Take my advice: *"Immerse yourselves exclusively in the now!"* Free yourselves of everything! Be *now* at *this* moment truly here—without thoughts, without concepts, and without impressions! Free yourselves of your conditionings! Don't cling to the past or to the future! Don't differentiate between enlightenment and nonenlightenment or between life and death! Die utterly into the moment. This is the way of directly and instantaneously grasping reality just as it is.

Be void of thoughts! For when thoughts arise, all things arise and therewith all problems; but when thoughts disappear, all problems disappear. *No thoughts and no concepts!* Just be yourselves—natural and spontaneous. But don't say to yourselves: "Here I am completely relaxed in the here and now," for no sooner have you done so than you've become fixated again, once more you've set a goal.

Mushotoku! "Without aim or striving for gain!" says Zen. Entirely absorb yourselves in the present moment. Here, now! and don't cling to anything, not even to silence, which will cause you to be irritated by any outside noise. If you hear a sound, then be the sound completely. Become the sound of a passing car, the song of a bird, or the bark of a dog. Whatever it is, everything is one. The perceiver, the process of perception, and the object of perception, all is a single reality.

And yet you could be overcome by fear with the thought: "If I am to leave everything so radically behind and so thoroughly become absorbed in the now, who knows what could happen? What if I suddenly experience such a drastic change in consciousness, a void in consciousness, that I'm sucked into a gaping abyss? What if I fall into a void from which I'm unable to return?"

Chinese Zen Master Po-chan (seventeenth century) says: "People should not worry so much about coming back from the state of mystical death, rather they should only concern themselves with going into it!" *That's* the sole point! The moment you let go, there is neither space nor time, neither life nor death.

An old Zen saying runs: "Bravely let go at the edge of the cliff. Resolute and full of trust throw yourself into the abyss. It's only after death that we begin to live. This alone is the truth."

What need a raindrop fear as it falls into the vast ocean and dissolves, thereby experiencing itself as the boundless ocean? Your fear of the void is caused solely by the fact that you haven't realized that your own mind is the void.

The problem comes down to your being afraid of fear! And that's an emotion. "When emotions arise, wisdom ceases," says Lin-chi. *Wisdom* is the reality of your Self-Being; it's the absolute *here,* the absolute *now!* Now is the beginning and the end. Recall the circle, the symbol for *shunyata,* which in Zen represents emptiness. It has no end and no beginning, no before and no after.

Meister Eckhart says: "Only one thing is necessary: detachment!" Be detached from all things. Die into the great death, and I guarantee you that this great death will reveal itself to be the *great life,* the *great joy* that will sweep in and liberate you completely, leaving nothing more to be attained.

The Eternal Tao

> The Tao that can be told is not the eternal Tao.
> The name that can be named is not the eternal name.
> The nameless is the beginning of heaven and earth.
> The named is the mother of the ten thousand things.
> Therefore ever desireless one beholds the mystery.
> Ever desiring one beholds only limitation.
> —Lao-tzu, sixth century B.C.

"The Tao that can be told is not the eternal Tao."

Anything we could say about Tao would fall short of the essential. Elsewhere in the *Tao te Ching,* Lao-tzu says, "It has no name, but for lack of a name I call it Tao." What is Tao? Tao is the absolute! In addition, *Tao* means "way," not only in the sense of a path one follows, as most people interpret it, but also in the sense of the reality that you yourself must become. The Chinese character for *Tao* is very old; it depicts a path and a foot to show that it is the path one follows. But Zen also tells us: *"The way and the aim are one."* Tao as the path you follow and Tao as the reality of your true essence are not two but *one.*

63

You must become the way, you must become Tao. Then you will experience Tao as the reality of the all-encompassing organic whole. This whole manifests itself as your true original being through the supposed multiplicity of a seemingly external phenomenal world.

"The Tao that can be told is not the eternal Tao.
The name that can be named is not the eternal name."

That which can be stated belongs to the realms of existence and nonexistence, to the categories of being and nonbeing. And "whoever reflects upon being or nonbeing loses life and limb," says Zen. These distinctions are no more than empty concepts. Behind them, however, lies the eternal that illuminates the entire universe with its light. It is that which it always is, was, and will be. Yet the Tao "that can be told," the expressible absolute (abstractly speaking) will always remain a shadow, an arbitrary conceptual designation. If I were to say God, Buddha, Christ, the absolute, or whatever, each of these terms would fall short of the essential. All efforts to force Tao into a conceptual configuration are like trying to capture the sky in a net. Tao is inconceivable and indefinable because to define means to set limits. Reality is right in front of you. A definition, on the other hand, is like an arrow that misses the target.

"The nameless is the beginning of heaven and earth."

The beginning of heaven and earth doesn't refer to the start of a timeline. It's not the beginning of a continuous sequence of events and happenings called the history of the world or the history of the universe that commenced at some point in time. There is no space or time, no multitude or sequence of movements, because everything is simultaneity having no beginning or end.

There is no beginning! It's all just the erroneous perception of discriminating, conceptual thinking. The nameless is *beginningless,* which is the beginning of heaven and earth. And the beginningless is also the endless, which is why Christ says, "I am the Alpha and the Omega!" In other words: "I am the beginning and the end. I am *eternity.*"

"The named is the mother of the ten thousand things."

The process of the mind's consciousness in the direction of existence leads to the perception of a spatial world of individuation. The moment conceptual fixation arises, even if it's only the faintest hint of an initial impulse, limits appear. It's like looking at the world through the end of a straw that limits your vision. This is the dualistic outlook through which the reality of the all-encompassing organic whole, the boundless expanse of the One Mind, is contracted to a microcosmic partial aspect of the cosmic Mind. In this manner, consciousness is contracted into the pseudo-existence of the ego.

But because everything is the One Mind besides which nothing exists, the named is identical in essence yet different in manifestation to the nameless. The named is conceptual fixation and thereby the mother of the ten thousand things. It brings all things into existence, causing the illusion of multiplicity to arise. That's why Lao-tzu says: *"Ever desiring one beholds only limitation."*

Desiring is wanting to possess, wanting to grasp and to cling because of *ignorance.* Where there is ignorance, there is also desire and hate. That's why *desire, hate,* and *ignorance* constitute the three basic evils from which samsara, the cycle of birth, old age, despair, sickness, pain, and death emerges. This basic condition is the root of all evil.

Ever desiring, one beholds only limitation because desire *sets* limits. Caused by ignorance, it generates further ignorance, and the veil of *maya,* the illusion of a manifold external phenomenal world, becomes increasingly more dense. You find yourselves caught in the web of desire, hate, and ignorance. The more you attempt to liberate yourselves, the more you become entangled and bound to this miserable, pitiable state of contracted consciousness.

That's limitation! Ever desiring one beholds only limitation. Now what I'm about to say could easily be misunderstood: Desire, specifically desire's inner driving force, is at the same time—and this is a very important point—the unconscious impulse toward the divine that dwells in every being.

All people seek but don't know what they are seeking. That's why Saint Augustine says: "Restless is our heart until it rests in you, oh God!" In your spiritual restlessness you rush about seeking here and there and don't know what you're seeking. You fail to realize that what you seek is actually the innermost driving force of your search itself. It's your true self over which the delusion of an ego and its experienced world is superimposed. Projected by desire, hate, and ignorance, this delusion obscures the reality of your original being.

All desire, in other words, all external seeking is actually a misunderstanding of that which you actually seek. You seek externally for something that can only be found within. The heart is restless, yet the heart rests in God when it realizes that God rests in it.

The clear light of the Mind shines at the heart's innermost place. Yet constant desire beholds the external only and constructs limitation. Through desire, you bind yourselves to your self-created limitation. This is how you give rise to the illusion of an independent, self-existing individuality, which is no other than limitation.

Let's now go back to Lao-tzu's statement. We first commented on the following statement in order to better understand the foregoing.

"Ever desireless one beholds the mystery."

To be "ever desireless" is to let go, but not in the sense of something you do, rather, in the sense of something you let happen. Meister Eckhart says: *"God works and I come into being."* In order for God to work in us, we are required to not work. As long as we do the work and with the help of conceptual thinking attempt to understand the mystery of being, God does not work! He says: "Great, fantastic, how wonderfully wise you are with all your knowledge and action. If you believe that you can do it yourself, fine. Have a go at it. I won't stand in your way."

"Ever desireless one beholds the mystery." If you don't desire but instead abide in nondesire and leave things the way they are, then you don't limit, you don't fixate, nor do you have any fixed perceptions. In other words, you no longer see the world through the dualistic perspective of acceptance and denial. You're free of your old accustomed patterns of behavior and modes of thought. You're free of your bygone memories of a dead past and your fears for the future. Everything is good just the way it is. "Every day is a good day," as Zen would say. Thus you proceed through all the ups and downs of life without losing a moment's thought over the right or wrong of the situation.

The only thing that matters is that you have the courage to let go and not become impatient if something doesn't happen right away, something magnificent such as a wonderful vision or if a divine light doesn't suddenly burst forth and fill you through and through with boundless wisdom. As long as you remain in a state of expectation in which you endeavor to let go in order to attain a goal, you're only fooling yourselves. When you say, "Yes, I've let everything go. I'm totally immersed in nondoing and nonthinking and I expect nothing," but secretly you are waiting for something to happen, then you haven't truly let go.

True letting go means dying. Everything must become as nothing, everything must become mu, *nothing!*—absolutely nothing. Become this nothing, and you'll discover your true face before your birth.

Love and Surrender

At the request of several students, I'd like to speak today about love and surrender.

There are two forms of love: love in the form of *having* and love in the form of *being*. Love in the form of *having* is love that manifests itself in a quick emotional stirring, in an impulse. Here's an example. While walking in a meadow you come upon a beautiful flower. You pick the flower and take it home with you because you're in love with the flower. At home you put it in a vase, and two or three days later you throw it in the trash. This is love in the form of having, which is not really love at all but the desire of the ego misinterpreted as love. You see an object, desire it, and want to grasp it. In other words, you want to *have* the object of desire.

It's quite different with love in the form of *being, pure* love. Pure love is love in the form of the all-encompassing whole. It doesn't get stuck in an emotional impulse. It's love that doesn't seek to grasp or own. Instead it does the opposite—*it surrenders itself,* just as does the moth that sees an open flame and flies into it. It dies into the object of love. Love is *oneness.* Love is non-duality. Love knows no separation. Meister Eckhart speaks of this true divine love when he says: "The eye with which I see God and the eye with which God sees me is one eye, one seeing, one knowing, and one loving." All duality is dissolved.

Love is the all-encompassing organic whole that contains everything within it. But when a person egocentrically withdraws from the whole, from the universal entirety, by calling attention to himself or herself and feeling important, that person withdraws from love. Duality, or division, is separation, and separation arises through greed, hate, and delusion; or we could say through desire, aggression, and ignorance.

Love surrenders itself. It's the key moment in the Passion of Christ. It's the love of God for humankind and of humankind for God. Divine love that gives of itself so radically is manifested in human love for the divine, where human and divine are experienced as one and there is no ego or self-will. For that reason Christ says in the garden of Gethsemane: "Father, if you will, let this cup pass from me; nevertheless not what I will, but what *you* will!"

This surrender culminates on the cross in the radical self-dissolution of Jesus the man. The attitude of the crucified Jesus is the attitude of total devotion of humankind to God, of the creaturely to the divine. At the same time it's the all-encompassing divine love that embraces the entire universe with open arms. On the cross, human love unites with divine love. And this love is radical and unwavering. "Die ere you die, so that you will not die, when you die!" says Silesius. Perfected in Christ's Passion on the cross, this is the *mystical death*.

At this point on the cross Jesus cries out the words that have confused many a Christian mind: "*Eli, Eli, lama sabachthani?*" These words mean: "My God, my God, why have you forsaken me?" Most theologians interpret this statement as a show of Jesus's humanity and helplessness as he hangs on the cross. In his hour of need, he feels so forsaken by the God he so trusted that in despair and fear of death he cries out: "My God, my God, why have you forsaken me?"

But the mystical significance, the truth behind the words, is altogether different. When Jesus cries out: "My God, my God, why have you forsaken me?" it's altogether different from if he had said: "Oh my, oh my, here I hang with hands and feet nailed to a cross. I trusted in a higher power that probably doesn't exist. It's all been a waste; I've been taken in by a fraud."

No, that's not what he says. Instead he appeals directly to divine reality and says: "My God, my God, why have you forsaken me?" Only one who is utterly certain of the existence of divine reality would address it in this manner. Nobody would address such words to someone who's existence he or she doubted—and certainly not Jesus. The words of the dying Jesus, "why have you forsaken me?" are unquestionably a cry of abandonment, but they're not words that doubt the existence of divine reality. For when Jesus cries: "My God, my God, why have you forsaken me?" at the same time he underlines his *irrefutable faith* in that which he feels has abandoned him.

At the moment of mystical death, the process of releasing yourself from space and time, you will find yourselves in the dark night of the mind and senses. You no longer have the one (the world), and you have yet to gain the other (the absolute), and this is a special state of spiritual vacuum. In this predicament of being abandoned, great trust in the absolute is necessary.

"Why have you forsaken me?" is a koan for humankind. It's a call to follow. Just as Jesus says to a follower: "Come and follow me!" "Wait a minute, not so fast," says the follower. "My father has died and first I must bury him." And Jesus responds: "I say to you, let the dead bury their own and follow me!" [The Master cracks his wooden sticks together.] *Now!!!* Not later on, not tomorrow or the day after tomorrow, for only now exists. Tomorrow and the day after tomorrow are only thoughts, empty concepts, just as are the ten thousand other empty concepts that you have in your heads.

Free yourselves of everything! Radically! Leave everything behind you! This is the dark night of the soul and the senses, as the Christian mystics say. This is where great trust in God is indispensable. The situation on the cross also shows this to us. In the Holy Scriptures we read: "There was a darkness over all the land and Jesus cried, 'Father, into your hands I commend my spirit.' He then bowed his head to the side and gave up his spirit. And behold, the earth quaked and the veil of the temple was torn in two from top to bottom, releasing the Holy of Holies."

This passage is not a mere historical account of some external event. Indeed, everything described in the Scriptures relates to the maturation process of the soul. You must not forget this. The moment you surrender yourselves to the absolute and die into the great death, the great darkness will come. Everything will melt away, all of your conditionings, all of your deep-rooted concepts and values. The veil of the temple, the *veil of maya,* the illusion of space and time, of old age, despair, sickness, pain, and death, is torn in two. Everything dissolves away and sets the Holy of Holies free. The Holy of Holies is your *true face* before your birth, the Self-Being reality that you always were and will be.

You are the temple. "Do you not know that you are the temple of the Holy Spirit?" asks Paul. Therefore, clear everything out of the temple, all conditionings and lifeless concepts, all the programming and slogans that you've drummed into your heads and had drummed into your heads by others over the course of your lifetime. Throw it all out! Get rid of it! Be like Jesus who goes into the temple, turns over the tables, and chases out the money changers and pigeon sellers with the cry: "Get out! You have turned my Father's house into a den of thieves. Away with you!" And then the temple is silent.

Once it is finally silent in the ground of the soul, the divine WORD, which speaks itself in the cave of the heart, will reveal itself. For as long as the soul has strange guests, as long as there is still something in you in the form of accepting and rejecting, right and wrong, and this, that, and the other thing, you cannot hear the WORD. This WORD is the divine reality which the Upanishads call "the one without a second." And being "the one without a second," it tolerates nothing beside it. As long as a single thing remains in the ground of the soul—be it but a tiny particle of a speck dust—you'll continue to be heavens apart from divine reality.

The thoroughness of self-dissolution and self-surrender to the divine abyss, which reveals itself to be the fullness of divine being, is the radical nature of divine love in its totality. That's the reason John says: "God is love, and he who abides in love abides in God and God in him." God is love—the all-encompassing whole. And whoever abides in this love, in this whole, in this nonduality, in this nonseparation, abides in divine reality. But the moment you take anything away, believing that it doesn't belong to the total harmony of divine being, you leave love behind. You lose love.

Yin and yang, life and death, beautiful and ugly, good and bad, everything is the organic totality of being. The connection, meaning the reciprocal causation and mutual penetration of yin and yang, is the working of Tao. Tao flows like water. And if you don't stand in opposition to anything, regardless of what it is, then you are in flow with the whole, in accord with Tao. And thus you dwell in the great divine love. "This love is as strong as death!" Just as death deprives you of everything and destroys everything, so does love. Whoever abides in the great divine love will experience everything as divine love, or in the words of Meister Eckhart: "Everything will become nothing but God to this person." Wherever this person goes or wherever this person lingers, divine reality is the only thing this person sees!

When you abide in love, in the *divine love* of which John speaks, you are beyond life and death. For everything is *one*. The whole universe, coming and going, birth and death—all of life, everything, regardless of what it is, is the fullness of divine being. And if you live *in* and *of* this fullness of divine being, you're free of worries and fear.

Death is no longer something that will happen one day, tearing you away from a pleasurable state of existence and hurling you down into a dark empty nothing. Much more, it simply reveals the other side of being—the reality of your birthless and deathless self-nature. Yin and yang are not opposites but, rather, *complements*—polarities. For everything is one, and one is the all-encompassing whole that contains everything within it.

So don't get stuck in accepting and rejecting; instead leave everything just as it is. Surrender yourselves to divine love, have great trust, and everything is good.

The Finger Is Not the Moon

E ach religion, each philosophy can only be considered a means of assistance, a "finger that points to the moon," as the *Lankavatara Sutra* says. It's like the trap we use to catch a fish. Once the fish is caught, we no longer need the trap.

You make a big fuss about all of the different ways and methods of acquiring something that you'll never be able to gain. Zen Master Huang-po therefore says: "That there is nothing which can be attained is not idle talk; it is the highest truth." You seek something that you'll never be able to find because you've never lost it. It's just like the old Indian parable about the man wearing a headband with a pearl on it who suddenly thinks that he has lost his pearl. He runs around from place to place, from town to town, from country to country, searching for his pearl until finally he looks in the mirror and realizes it was with him the whole time: He'd never lost it. It's just a matter of *realization*, not a matter of attainment.

Really look, leave everything just as it is, stop running about like frightened chickens, and see things the way they are! When you leave everything just as it is, you no longer try to make everything fit into the mold of conceptual fixation, the mold of your old accustomed way of viewing things. You no longer distort situations and things with your recollections, with the contents of your memory of a dead past, and you no longer mistake your projections for the things themselves.

Say one night in the moonlight you spot a rope lying alongside a path, and in a state of panic you project the thought of a snake onto it. Overcome with fear, you turn and run away. Yet the next day in the sunshine you pass along the same way and you see the snake was only a rope. The sunlight of unobstructed realization shows you the truth and enables you to see things as they are. Nothing is projected, everything is clear, and everything is good. "Every day is a good day," says Zen. Every situation is a wonderful situation because every situation is the revelation of divine reality.

Even one thought of grasping and you are caught by desire. Even one thought of rejecting and you are filled with anger and hate. That's why I say again and again: The true attitude of mind is one of inner equanimity. You abide within yourselves while moving about in a world of supposed multiplicity, and you leave things just as they are. In other words, it's incorrect to conceptualize the world and to categorize it in terms of good or not good. It's incorrect to believe that the world is a hindrance to following the "spiritual path." It's incorrect to believe that the world amounts to chasing after material possessions, fame, prestige, and success; and that therefore these must be avoided. That's one perspective. However, a perspective is only a single point of view to the exclusion of other points of view. It means looking through the end of the drinking straw of contracted consciousness. The vast expanse of the Mind of suchness is contracted into a microcosmic partial aspect—the point of view of the ego.

The world, meaning every situation in which you find yourselves in life, is neither good nor bad, neither right nor wrong. Your conditioned perspectives cause you to project all possible notions onto that which you see, onto all that you encounter. You project your old worn-out recollections, the ancient contents of a lifeless memory, onto the situation and react in an accustomed manner with favor or disfavor, convinced that things really are as they appear to you. Take the following example: You see a young woman, beautiful and pure as a flower. However, feelings of lust cause you to project sexual desires onto that person, and in the end all you see is a sex object. That's not the world as it is. What you experience is not suchness, but yourself in your ego-delusion.

The ego projects and puts together its own world. The world of the ego is no more than an endless coming and going of wishes and fears, thoughts and feelings, and is therefore the cycle of birth and death that we call *samsara*. The cycle of birth and death is merely a psychical projection of consciousness. In order to be able to recognize reality as it is, you first must awaken from your habitual misinterpretations and the resulting misperceptions. Then you will become the *tathagata*, the thus-come one, who sees things the way they are.

Getting to this point requires the spiritual guidance of an enlightened master. When you begin your search for a master in today's giant maze of spiritual paths, you will encounter thousands upon thousands of self-proclaimed masters. Such pseudo-gurus only parrot what they have read or heard from others. Only one who has awakened to the original condition of his being is a true master; only he has the authority to teach.

Whoever presumes to talk about enlightenment without having experienced it himself is like a blind person attempting to describe Michelangelo's ceiling painting of the Sistine Chapel.

Some of you might be thinking: "If there are really so few real masters, then most people must be lost." Keep in mind that there are also many *upaya* (aids), as they are termed by Buddhists. These are preparatory teachings that may also be taught by unenlightened teachers who act as guides and can at least bring students as far as they have come themselves. Then the student must find another teacher who has an even deeper understanding, until finally the student is adequately prepared for a *true* master. There are few, however, who are really ripe for the encounter with a master.

Many people have encountered a master and then turned away because they weren't able fully to realize that a *true enlightened master* stood before them. That's the way it is today, and that's the way it's always been, even back in the times of Christ and Buddha. Many people saw Buddha and turned their backs to him; they heard his wonderful teachings and said: "What nonsense." Many heard Jesus and said: "Who's that egomaniac who says he's the son of God? He's not clear in the head. What blasphemy; he can't be a true master." You must be ripe for a master. Meister Eckhart therefore urges us, "Climb higher, friend." This is how one surpasses the "double-tongued masters," as they are called in Zen.

Now let's go back to the beginning of our discussion. All philosophical and religious systems are only means of assistance and thus have little to do with reality itself, no more than the finger that points to the moon. All cerebral acrobatic speculation has nothing to do with reality, nothing at all!

What is it then? What is the truth? A logical question. The mind always thinks logically, and thus the answer it finds is logical, too. And precisely because the answer is logical, the answer is wrong, for all conceptual thinking is erroneous belief—we can spare ourselves the effort. Anything that can be conceptually expressed has nothing to do with reality, which is nameless and formless. The intellect thinks solely in terms of pairs of opposing concepts and says: "If it's not this, then it must be that. If it's not yang, it must be yin; and if it's not yin, it must be yang." Or, "If it's not movement, then of course it must be stillness." But it's neither one nor the other. That's why Buddha says of the absolute: "One cannot say that it is, and one cannot say that it is not. One cannot say that it is and is not, and one also cannot say that it neither is nor is not." This is the fourfold Buddhist negation. Zen Master Mumon expresses it his own way. He sweeps everything aside so that the only thing remaining is mu, *nothing*:

> *MU MU MU MU MU*
> *MU MU MU MU MU*
> *MU MU MU MU MU*
> *MU MU MU MU MU*

Nothing is real, nothing exists, everything is a dream without the slightest reality. Still you cling to the notion that behind this nothing is something, a perceiver, an observer behind the experience. Your *clinging* is precisely what causes you to obscure this observer behind all experiences, your true self, without your even knowing. You believe that what you perceive right now is your true self, but it's really only the ego. The ego is not a thing, a person, or a being; the ego is an occurrence, a process. Specifically, it's the process of identification, of grasping. It's also called *ahamkara*, which means "the process of ego-projection, the ego-maker, or *ego-delusion*." Because this is so, the ego is not something to which you can give a deathblow.

There is much talk these days about killing the ego, but because no ego exists, there is nothing to kill. The sole thing you could and should put to death is the *delusion* of an ego. And this can only be accomplished by putting an end to the process that *gives rise* to ego-delusion. But just what is this process? It's the process of constant, perpetual accepting and rejecting, the process of discrimination. According to the biblical tradition, this process began in the Garden of Eden. God told humankind not to eat from the tree of knowledge—of discrimination between good and evil—or he would run them out of paradise. And so it happened, which is why you're sitting here right now. Nevertheless, you still are in paradise. Nothing ever happened. It's just that the veil of acceptance and rejection has been draped over the pure perception of suchness, and you can only see the projection of your ignorance while believing "This is how the world is."

"When thoughts arise, then do all things arise," says Huang-po, "and when thoughts vanish, then do all things vanish." When thoughts arise, then do all problems arise; and when thoughts vanish, then do all problems vanish. Imagine for a moment that you have a problem—any problem, whatever it may be. Then suppose that while you are mulling over your problem, you suddenly get shot in the leg, and you now have a bullet lodged there. Are you still thinking about your problem?

Zen Master Pai-chang, Huang-po's master, gives us a wonderful remedy. He says: "When your mind moves, do not follow it and it will detach itself from the movement. And when your mind rests upon something, do not follow it and it will detach itself from that upon which it rests." If you truly want to enter the realm of enlightenment, then it is necessary for you to clear out your mind so that it is as empty as a vacant room. Detach yourselves from your old views and from all grasping. Stop trying to understand reality through the use of conceptual thinking, and your false ideas and suppositions will dissolve of themselves. If you follow these instructions, then you are on the path to enlightenment.

The Original Condition
of the Mind

*When someone in his own mind recalls
the original condition of his Mind,
then all deceptive thoughts dissolve away on their own
into the realm of the ultimate reality.*
—Mahamudra Master Milarepa, twelfth century

These words make sufficiently clear that the individual mind does not necessarily abide in the direct experience of its Self-Being, its original condition. Nevertheless, the *individual* mind is not separate from this original condition, which is the *One Mind*.

Our drinking straw demonstration makes a good analogy. Take a straw, aim it in the direction of the sky, and look through the end of it. The endless expanse of the sky is like the boundless expanse of the One Mind. But because of the fixation of restricting, dualistic thinking, your perception is reduced to a microcosmic, partial aspect of the cosmic Mind. So there you are in a state of contracted consciousness, of supposed individuality, a subjective entity that perceives itself as separate from everything it sees and experiences. You look through the straw, and the small point inside the circle is your individual mind. The periphery of the circle represents the existence factors *(skandhas)* that create the illusion of personality. The existence factors are corporeality or form, sensations, perceptions, mental formations, and consciousness.

"Form" *(rupa skandha)* includes every form that we perceive, touch, and see; "sensations" *(vedana skandha)* are our reactions to an object: favor, disfavor, or indifference; "perception" *(samjna skandha)* includes seeing, hearing, smelling, touching, and tasting; "mental formations" *(samskara skandha)* are all impulses of will, all intellectual impulses of the mind, thought processes, thought contents, impressions, and concepts; "consciousness" *(vijnana skandha)* is not to be confused with the ultimate, unchanging entity behind all experience, as many people think—rather, according to Buddhist teachings, it stands for the formation of consciousness, *vijnana.*

Consciousness is a process. It's not the reality underlying your experiences. Consciousness is an event, a chain of conscious moments that follow one after the other. Buddhist psychology also refers to *flashes of consciousness* that give rise to the illusion of continuous, uninterrupted consciousness. It's equivalent to a sequence of pictures on film that, when projected onto a screen, creates the illusion of solid objects and movement. We think we're looking at a river, for example, but what we actually see are hundreds of pictures run off in sequence—moments of consciousness, that is to say, a chain of moments of existence and combinations thereof.

The illusion of personality is created by the interplay of the five existence factors, the skandhas. Skandhas are inconstant and have no real being. They are merely appearance; they are a process. All depends on what has gone before. Nothing existents in and of itself; everything is an occurrence in the form of an illusion of phenomena brought forth by what has gone prior.

The foundation of Buddhist philosophy and psychology is the truth of *pratitya samutpada,* or interdependent arising (also called conditional nexus). Everything we perceive in the universe arises through dependence on something else, and therefore everything has a beginning—and that which has a beginning also has an end. However, beginning and end are purely illusory. They occur within the confines of a moment of time that, together with space, has no reality. Time and space are *categories of consciousness,* which means that they are given conditions through which human consciousness perceives a supposed exterior world. In truth, everything is merely an impression, an idea, and therefore lacks its own being.

We won't delve too deeply into the psychology of perception here because it would take too much time. The essential thing to know and understand is that the world as we perceive it is only a projection of consciousness, which is not a thing in and of itself but, rather, a process. Perceptions, notions, and thoughts cannot be differentiated from the thinker because all thoughts are illusory, as is the one who thinks them. The thinker, too, is just a *process*—he or she has no real being.

Let's return to Milarepa's statement: "When someone in his own mind recalls the original condition of his Mind . . ." The original condition of the Mind is the *reality* behind all experience. It's like the screen on which the pictures, movements, colors, and forms of a film are projected. If you're able to perceive this reality, then you're able to perceive your Mind's original condition and ". . . all deceptive thoughts dissolve away on their own into the realm of the ultimate reality."

The deceptive thoughts referred to here indicate the entire ego process and at the same time the process that consolidates and sustains the skandhas and thereby samsara.

The skandhas and samsara are *one* process. However, the individual mind is not separate from the reality of the One Mind. The moment the mind's boundary falls, constricted consciousness, which is pseudo-individuality together with its perceived world, evaporates, and the boundless expanse of the Self-Mind reveals itself in the emptiness *(shunyata).* This is the *original condition of the Mind,* and this Mind is the same as the one that had enclosed itself within a self-made boundary and identified itself with it.

Freeing yourself of this boundary is not something you can do. It's not something you can accomplish through force of will. You can't wage war against the boundary because the more you fight it, the stronger it grows into a prison of the self. You end up locking yourself away in a prison of ignorance.

The original condition of the Mind is your true being, it's really your own mind. But wait, the sentence continues: "When someone in his own mind recalls the original condition of his Mind, then all deceptive thoughts dissolve on their own into the realm of the ultimate reality. There is no longer anyone who causes suffering, nor anyone who suffers." "When thoughts arise, then do all things arise," says Huang-po, "and when thoughts vanish, then do all things vanish." When all thoughts vanish, so too, do all samsaric formations or skandhas that generate pseudo-individuality. The ego evaporates, and thus there is no longer anyone who causes suffering. And if there is no longer anyone who causes suffering, there can be no suffering. Suffering never comes from without, but always from within.

The transitory nature of all worldly things that are pleasing to you will never cause you suffering provided you refrain from clinging to such things. Meister Eckhart says: "All suffering comes from love and attachment. So if I suffer on account of transitory things, then I and my heart have love and attachment for temporal things. Is it any wonder then that God permits me

84

to be rightly afflicted with loss and sorrow?" When you cling to what pleases you or what you imagine pleases you and then it's taken away from you, suffering arises. Yet the thing itself does not cause you to suffer. Suffering is brought on solely by attachment. Attachment is like petrifaction: it hardens, becomes rigid and inert. It's opposed to the flow of Tao.

Last time we heard from Huang-po's teacher, Zen Master Pai-chang: "When your mind moves, do not follow it and it will detach itself from the movement. And when your mind comes to rest upon something, do not follow it and it will detach itself from that upon which it rests." This is true *satipatthana*, as it is called in Buddhism—the realization of mindfulness. And the mental attitude of the realization of mindfulness is one of *wu-wei* and *wu-nien,* nondoing and nonthinking. In other words, let things happen, and leave things as they are so that events, situations, and things do not become fixated and your consciousness does not harden. As Lao-tzu says: "The hard and rigid dies a poor death."

Therefore, detach yourselves from your conditionings and from your identification with what you once experienced! Detach yourselves from all intellectual rubbish and from the shadows of a dead past, which are not worth losing even a single thought over, but nonetheless form the core of "Western psychology."

If it weren't for rummaging around in such refuse, there would be no "Western psychology"; there would be no "therapy." This is called bridling the horse at the tail and only leads to going around in circles. You can exert yourselves as much as you like and you can try using psychology to find a way out of this hopeless situation. Bewildered, you use all your might to attempt to escape, whereby you only entangle yourselves ever more in the creeping snarl of your self-made spiritual confusion. And so you remain caught in this spiritual chaos, this blindness; this prison of conditioning, these behavioral patterns and modes of thought. It's even possible that you'll wind up falling into a psychosis, which could become permanent.

That's why I say: *Free yourselves of everything!* But don't take this as a task for you to execute. If you abide in *suchness* as you sit before me right now, then in fact you're abiding in your original condition. This means that you leave things the way they are and you quit clinging to the idea of a past and a future, which are merely thoughts.

Past, present, and future are like leaves that blow by the window of our consciousness in the autumn wind—they are quickly gone. Buddhism refers to past, present, and future as the foundation of the three worlds. Even a single short instant, a quick snap of the fingers, contains these three worlds. Only *now* is reality. "Here and now!" [The Master cracks his wooden sticks together.] Suchness, *tathata.* That is the original condition of the Mind.

It's where there is no I and there is no you; there is no coming or going, no before and no after. There is only *now.* This now is the divine reality described by Meister Eckhart with the words: "God is the absolute *now.*" It's nonduality, the absolute present, the *all-encompassing totality of being.*

You need not seek anywhere; you need not go anywhere. Where could you go to seek the reality of your being that you yourself are? Where would you find the "divine light that shines in the darkness," to use the words of the prologue to the Gospel of John; where would you find it besides in the *cave of the heart, in yourself?*

Nevertheless, one thought, then another brings forth feelings, mental formations, and impressions. Then come desire, hate, and blindness, out of which samsara arises. All of this obscures the true condition of the Mind, making it impossible for us to recognize the divine light that shines in the darkness.

Using a thought process or your capacity for intellectual understanding in trying to find this divine light is like trying to find a burning candle in a great hall by turning on all the lights. It must be dark. Mu! Nothing! Nondesire, nonthinking. Finally, have the courage to leave everything just as it is. This is the great faith, *shraddha,* of which Buddhism speaks.

It's important that you awaken this great faith within yourselves. Instead of relying on yourselves, on your intellectual capabilities, abide in wu-wei, in nondoing, and give the reality of the Universal Mind a chance to work. *Wu-wei* means to abide in nondoing in such a way as to allow Tao to work through us. Meister Eckhart says: "God works and I come into being!"

You can't force anything, for the sole reason that there is nothing to achieve. As soon as you believe that there is something to achieve, some goal to attain, you're on the verge of throwing yourselves into the hell of the hundred thousand demons. Yet these demons are none other than your own projections. They are the self-generated inner tensions that come from chasing after a wishful notion that only exists in your head. Inner tension is impeded desire.

Everything is here Now! [The Master stomps his staff on the floor.] Now!!! You lack nothing. Not the least little thing. So what brings you to me? What do you want from me? Where does the shoe pinch? Sons and daughters of the Most High, manifestations of divine reality: You are "absolute *being,* boundless *consciousness,* infinite *bliss,*" as it says in the Upanishads. That alone is what you are. All else is bubbles, dreams, and shadows.

"When someone in his own mind recalls the original condition of his Mind, then all deceptive thoughts dissolve away on their own into the realm of the ultimate reality. There is no longer anyone who causes suffering, nor anyone who suffers. The most exhaustive study of the sutras [the sacred scriptures of Buddhism] teaches us no more than this." In the words of Huang-po: "All the buddhas and all sentient beings are nothing but the One Mind, beside which nothing exists. This Mind, which is without beginning, is unborn and indestructible."

And in the words of *Advaita-Vedanta:* *"Tat tvam asi,"* that you are.

Don't forget! Never forget who you really are! And don't mistake yourselves for that which you once experienced. Don't confuse yourselves with what you think you once were, how you saw yourselves in your ignorance, and how others saw you. All of that has no more reality than a dream that you dreamed twenty years ago.

The past [the Master holds up a wooden stick] and the future [the Master holds up another wooden stick]—two things: the past and the future. "Realities," everyone would say. But the past and the future are just illusions. [A crack of the sticks.] *Only one!* Now! That's it!

The True Way

A student of Zen comes to Zen Master Nansen and asks him, "What is the true way?" The Master replies, "The everyday way is the true way." The student continues, "Can one learn the way?" The Master answers, "The more you learn, the more you distance yourself from the way." Thereupon the student asks, "If the way cannot be approached through learning, how can one recognize it?" Master Nansen speaks: "The way is not something visible, nor is the way something invisible. It is not recognizable and not unrecognizable. Do not seek it, do not learn it, do not name it. Be as vast and as open as the sky and you are on the way."

"What is the true way?" This is the student's question. It means: "What is the truth, what is the meaning of all being, and what is the way to enlightenment?" And the Master replies, "The everyday way is the true way." This statement is the foundation of Zen.

The everyday way. Everything you encounter, regardless of what it is, is the true way with no differentiation between sacred and nonsacred, religious and nonreligious, spiritual and nonspiritual. The true way is the reality that lies at the ground of everything, that reveals itself in everything. Everything is wonderful; everything is fine just the way it is. And if things weren't the way they are, that would be fine, too. Every differentiation is a deviation from reality. This thought is often found in the words of Meister Eckhart. Take the following, for example.

"A person walks across a field and knows God, or he is in the church and knows God. If he knows God more because he abides at a quiet place, then it is a result of his own inadequacy and no fault of God. God is equally in all things and in all places and is willing to give himself in the same way, thus giving his whole being."

Experience divine reality in all things and in all places, in the midst of a crowd, among your fellow human beings, *everywhere,* regardless of the situation—smack-dab in the midst of everyday living. This is the "everyday way," and the everyday way is the *true way.*

Most people assume the way is something extraordinary, and so off they go to search for a very special way, thinking: "Somewhere there must be a secret, a specific path, a certain golden thread; when we find it, then we'll have it." But that's making a big mistake. You can seek as long as you like, but anything you could possibly find would be no more than the product of conceptual, differentiating thought. Regardless of the hue or form of religion or philosophy it takes, it can't be reality.

The student in our example who comes to Zen Master Nansen also believes that the way is something special. That's why he asks: "Can one learn the way?" He wants to have a particular method, a system. He wants to have something tangible to use. But Master Nansen replies: "The more you learn, the more you distance yourself from the way."

Generally, but especially to Western thinking, this statement makes absolutely no sense because in everyday life the rule is The more you learn, the more you know. The more knowledge you accumulate about something, the more familiar you will become with it and the more you will understand it. But take my word, it's possible for someone to read and memorize everything ever written about Zen and still not come even a hair's breadth closer to the truth of Zen. This is because the more you learn, the more you are in danger of clinging to concepts and ideas. The more knowledge of philosophical works you amass, the more distance you will put between yourselves and your inner reality.

Master Nansen's student still doesn't get it, and he goes on to ask, "If the way cannot be approached through learning, how can one recognize it?" And the Master says:

> *"The way is not something visible,*
> *nor is the way something invisible.*
> *It is not recognizable and not unrecognizable.*
> *Do not seek it, do not learn it, do not name it.*
> *Be as vast and as open as the sky*
> *and you are on the way."*

A magnificent answer. It contains the entire essence of Zen. Tao, the way, is not something visible. But no sooner is this said then you begin to reason: "If it's not something visible, well fine, then it must be invisible, something that I'm unable to perceive." Master Nansen swiftly sweeps this thought away too by adding: "Nor is the way something invisible." It's neither this nor that. We can't so much as say that the way, Tao, *is*—that it has being. We also can't say that it is not. Gautama Buddha says: "One cannot say that it is, and one cannot say that it is not. One cannot say that it is and is not, and one also cannot say that it neither is nor is not." In other words, anything I could say about it would fall short of the essential.

> *"It is not recognizable and not unrecognizable. Do not*
> *seek it, do not learn it, do not name it."*

To seek something that is your own reality, something that sustains and unceasingly surrounds and fills you, is meaningless.

Therefore: "Be as vast and as open as the sky and you are on the way."

If you are as vast and as open as the sky, this attitude of mind will accompany you in the midst of everyday life. Regardless of where you are, regardless of what events take place, you are "as vast and empty as the sky," which makes you transparent and translucent. You are beyond accepting and rejecting, and in the thick of the hustle and bustle of the world you abide in the cheerful serenity of the Mind.

Another student once came to Zen Master Nansen and asked him, "Did the ancients have any secret teaching that I do not yet know?" "Yes," said Master Nansen. The student eagerly went on to ask, "What is this teaching?" The Master responded, "It's not the heart, it's not Buddha, it's nothing at all."

For this reason I would like to close today's lecture with the advice of Zen Master Nansen: "Be as vast and as open as the sky and you are on the way!"

Trust Yourself

Students today lack self-confidence; they should not seek externally. As long as you continue to rely upon the methods of the ancient masters, you will never be able to distinguish between true and false.
—Zen Master Lin-chi, ninth century

The methods of the ancient masters are good, you could even say great. But at the same time you mustn't forget that the reality you seek in the scriptures—the statements of the ancient masters—is your own being. You seek something that you yourselves are, something that you've never lost. That's what Lin-chi means when he begins with the words: "Students today lack self-confidence; they should not seek externally." Chinese Zen Master Fen-yang (eleventh century) said: "Few people believe their own mind is buddha. Most do not take this seriously and therefore are cramped. They are wrapped up in illusions, cravings, resentments, and other afflictions, all because they love the cave of ignorance."

We each have our own special perspective, an understanding of what we study, of what we read or hear; nonetheless it never amounts to more than a limited point of view. The same goes for all external philosophies and religions.

Recall the old Indian tale of the five blind men who meet an elephant driver seated on an elephant's back. They call to him, "We're blind and don't know what an elephant looks like. May we touch and feel your elephant in order to find out?" "As you wish," says the elephant driver. The first man feels the trunk and exclaims, "Oh, it hadn't occurred to me that an elephant looks like a thick hose!" The second touches the elephant's ear and declares, "Oh my, the elephant looks like a big fan!" The third grabs hold of the tail and says, "Hey, the elephant looks like a thin rope!" The fourth examines the leg and proclaims, "The elephant looks like a tree stump! The fifth pats the elephant on the stomach and says, "You're all wrong. The elephant looks like a huge barrel!" Upon hearing this the elephant driver interrupts, "All of you are wrong. You've each grasped only a *part* of the whole, but no one has discerned what the elephant really looks like."

All statements of religion and philosophy should be understood in this light. Only once you dive directly into the ocean of wisdom yourselves, into the ocean of the *One Mind,* will you come to know the truth. If you want to know what water is, drink it! Or jump into the water! This is the way of Zen. Zen doesn't offer lengthy philosophical explanations. Zen says: "If you want to know how tea tastes, drink it! If you want to know how an apple tastes, take a bite! Then you will know how an apple tastes." That's Zen.

Zen always goes *straight* to the heart of the matter. Zen wastes no time with extraneous aesthetic argumentation or with any such acrobatic cerebral speculation. It doesn't heap up any intellectual rubbish. Zen—the word says it all—means "absorption." Absorption in the *One.* This explains Huang-po's saying: "Buddha and all sentient beings are nothing but the *One Mind,* beside which nothing exists." The last few words, "beside which nothing exists," are essential. The One Mind is the all-pervading entirety of all presumed multiplicity. All the waves on the surface of the ocean are the ocean itself. The waves' movement, the waves' various forms, the foam and bubbles on the surface—the entire confounding myriad of coming and going—is the one ocean.

Every perception of multiplicity is due to the mistaken perception of a dualistic consciousness, which further generates the delusion of individuality. The pseudo-individual, the ego, has no substantiality and no real being. It's not something that exists on its own. It's really just a process of identification with memories of a dead past, with old patterns of behavior, and countless notions and concepts. But you are not that. Nonetheless, you believe that's what you are and what everyone else is. Furthermore, you believe that what you perceive through your senses is the external world. What you perceive through your sense organs as an external world is only seemingly so, for in truth, space is no more than a *projection of your consciousness.* Because the prerequisite for perceiving something external is lacking, then every perception of something external is thus a process of *looking within.*

Everything is found *within.* But don't think of *within* as being the opposite of without, for it is the dimension *beyond* space and time. What you actually perceive is the spaceless and timeless dimension of the Mind, but you fail to recognize it as such because it is overshadowed by samskaras, the karmic driving forces. Karmic driving forces are the entire process of identification, the attachment and differentiation that I just finished describing. Taking this for the world, you say: "This is the world we experience, the world within which we are trapped. How can we possibly escape?" In fact, you're not trapped. The idea of being trapped is just a thought. You've stirred up a mind game, a *dream vision,* a web of maya. You've entangled yourselves in it and are unable to free yourselves.

Because everything is no more than a web of thoughts, freeing yourselves from it can only mean taking the sword of realization and slicing through the Gordian knot of your spiritual confusion. [The Master whacks his staff against the side table.] The problem is solved. Even better, the problem is not solved because there never was a problem. It was only an illusion!

What do you lack then? The only thing you lack is trust in yourselves. This trust is the indisputable belief in your own immanent divine reality. This belief matures into an absolute certainty that things are just as the enlightened masters— those who have awakened—of all times have proclaimed.

The master's words are fingers that point to the moon. The moon is reality, the finger is merely the guidepost. But you study the finger. You study the various systems of instruction, philosophies, and religions and take them for the truth. On the contrary, they're just worthless junk! Intellectual refuse! Nothing! The *moon,* not the finger, is the truth. Never forget this. The illumination of the Self-Mind beyond all speculation and perception, beyond the supposed external world, is the reality that you seek! This is the true condition of the boundless, ultramundane Mind. All else is illusion.

That's why you must leave everything behind! Let the dead bury their own and surrender yourselves to divine being! It's the only way! Zen Master Lin-chi says: "A righteous man discusses neither rulers nor rebels, neither right nor wrong, neither beauty nor wealth. He does not spend his days in discussion over empty words." He leaves things just as they are. The political factors of a world situation do not disturb him in the least. He does not differentiate between right and wrong and is not interested in beauty, wealth, possessions, or fashion; these things don't have the slightest meaning to him. They're simply reflections of your ignorance, of your fears and desires; reflections of attachment, aversion, and spiritual blindness (according to Buddha's teaching).

The reflections of a manifold world with all its problems amount to no more than shadows obscuring the reality of the Self-Mind. How can you escape? Certainly not by looking all over the place or by searching here and there.

[The Master stomps his staff on the floor.] *This is it!* Everything is here—now! It's here at this moment. If you absorb yourselves entirely in here and now, you will see your face before your birth, your unborn and undying *Self-Being.*

In today's esoteric entertainment market the expression "here and now" has become a catchphrase. "Here and now" can be found in almost every book belonging to the "esoteric wave." It can be found in the writings of American actresses and pop singers who call themselves spiritual masters and put in appearances everywhere, and in the books and workshops of psychologists and therapists. Everyone talks about "here and now." When you understand what this really means in Zen, then you'll realize that the esoteric "here and now" has little to do with it.

Here is now! That's all. The reality of your Self-Being does not know space and time; it is the absolute *here and now!* Do you hear it? [Silence.] Whoever has ears with which to hear, will hear. In Zen it is said: "To see with the ears and hear with the eyes is called true understanding." And Christ says: "They have eyes with which to see and they see not. They have ears with which to hear and they hear not."

Hear the thunder of silence! Zen Master Hakuin says: "If you clap two hands together, you produce a sound." [The Master hits two wooden sticks together.] "But tell me, what is the sound of one hand?" [The Master raises one stick in the air.]

It is neither being nor nonbeing. Neither hearing nor nonhearing. If you want to experience here and now, then you must die into here and now—here and now! This is the only way. This is the truth of Zen. That's all there is to say!

Free Yourself of Everything
Radical Guidance in the Spirit of Zen and Christian Mysticism
by Wolfgang Kopp
translated from the German by Barbara Wittenberg-Hasenauer

Intended for those who earnestly seek spiritual guidance, this book conveys the deepest wisdom of eastern and western mysticism. Drawing from his vast experience as a practicing meditation master, and using examples from the great masters of Zen and Christian mysticism, the author presents the fundamental elements necessary for a successful journey to inner freedom.

Wolfgang Kopp was a student of Soji Enku, Roshi. As Enku Roshi's dharma successor, he directs the Tao Ch'an Center in Wiesbaden, Germany.

ISBN: 0–8048–1989–0, 144 pages

Fundamentals of Mainstream Buddhism
by Eric Cheetham

Prepared by the distinguished Buddhist Society of London, this book aims to present the major topics of the first phase of Indian Buddhism, sometimes referred to as the Hinayana or "the Small Vehicle." The material is drawn from major texts and commentaries, translated from the Pali and Sanskrit languages.

Eric Cheetham is a scholar and lecturer at the Buddhist Society, London.

ISBN: 0–8048–3008–8, 224 pages

Two Arrows Meeting in Mid-Air
The Zen Koan
by John Daido Loori

Through a comprehensive introduction and twenty-one chapters centered on koans from classic collections and modern encounters, this book presents the relevance of koan study as it relates to modern Zen training. The author draws on his many dharma discourses to provide a detailed examination of each koan, connecting the contemporary reader to the traditional Zen lineages.

John Daido Loori is the spiritual leader and abbot of the Zen Mountain Monastery in Mt. Tremper, New York. Trained in koan Zen as well as in the subtle school of Master Dogen's Zen, he is a dharma heir to Hakuyu Taizan Maezumi, Roshi.

ISBN: 0–8048–3012–6, 392 pages

The Whole World is a Single Flower
365 Kong-ans for Everyday Life
by Zen Master Seung Sahn
Foreword by Stephen Mitchell

"One of the greatest collections of koans since the dawn of Zen in the West."
—*Tricycle, The Buddhist Review*

Korean Zen Master Seung Sahn provides 365 kong-ans (koans), which are practice for life—practice for answering both the practical and profound questions that arise every day. The kong-ans come from traditional Chinese and Korean Zen as well as from Lao-tzu and the Christian tradition. Master Seung Sahn provides additional questions and commentary to each kong-an which will serve as guideposts on the reader's path to enlightenment.

ISBN: 0–8048–1782–0, 272 pages

For further information and to order copies of any of these
titles please visit your local bookstore, or write to:

Charles E. Tuttle Co., Inc.
RR1 box 231-5
North Clarendon, VT 05759–9700, USA

or call toll-free within the United States 1–800–526–2778
outside of the United States call 802–773–8930